ABORTION
AND THE SENSELESS ASSAULT ON
REPRODUCTIVE RIGHTS

Based on
Gross Judicial Ignorance Willful Arrogance
and a Lack of Court Ethics

DORRIS S. WOODS, PHD
(Retired RN, Clinical Specialist)

**ABORTION AND THE SENSELESS ASSAULT
ON REPRODUCTIVE RIGHTS**

Copyright © 2024 Dr. Dr. Dorris Woods

Because of the dynamic nature of the Internet, any web addresses or links contained in this book may have changed since publication and may no longer be valid. The views expressed in this work are solely those of the author and do not necessarily reflect the views of the publisher, and the publisher hereby disclaims any responsibility for them.

Library of Congress Control Number:	2023950600
Paperback:	978-1-961119-60-4
eBook:	9781961119-61-1

Printed in the United States of America

CONTENTS

DEDICATED TO:

My longtime friend,
Dr. Dorothy Ehrhart-Morrison
who encouraged me to "spread my wings,"
and
the thousands of women who have been needlessly
traumatized mentally, physically, and emotionally
by the overturning of Roe
and
physicians that I made a pledge before God to support,
who have had medical decisions taken away from you and
put into the hands of courts, judges, and politicians.

ACKNOWLEDGMENTS

I owe a debt of gratitude to all who impacted the writing of this book. I am especially grateful to those who took the time to participate in the survey; your point of view means a lot to me.

Thanks to my neighbors, Mary Lang and Edie Levinson, for clipping articles. And especially to Mary Lang for writing.

A special thanks to Barbara Allen of BA Writers' Services for efficiently organizing the survey and processing the manuscript for publication. You are indispensable.

FOREWORD

It is beyond comprehension that a Supreme Court justice—someone at the apex of the United States judicial system could render a decision about a procedure about which he obviously knows nothing about its ramifications.

Justice Alito would have done himself a favor, as well as millions of women if he had told himself: "I don't know nothing' about birthing' no baby!" as Hattie McDaniel said in *Gone With the Wind.* Common sense should have directed him to consult experts in the field of obstetrics/gynecology. Also, there were huge protest marches after the "leak". He neglected to listen to them.

Now we know that religion was not the only motivation for his opinion. We are not a nation of Catholics as many women have pointed out. Then, too, not all Catholic women like having their reproductive freedom taken away. In Chapter Five, Women Having Their Say, one of the survey participants wrote, "Consequences of their decisions should be widely publicized, i.e., before a vote. Each justice should explain the reasoning for his or her decision. Too many members base their decisions on their own religious backgrounds." According to him, he did not want to appear intimidated by the leak.

As the legal challenges to abortion bans have increased, so have media accounts of undue human suffering. Consider the incident involving a young married woman in Lakeland, Florida. She went to her doctor with her second pregnancy. After prenatal examinations were done, she was told the fetus had Potter's syndrome and should be aborted.

Potter's syndrome is a condition in utero where the amniotic fluid is insufficient for a healthy environment to develop. The parents wanted the abortion, but doctors feared legal retaliation. So, the mother had no choice but to carry the fetus to term, knowing it would not survive. She and her husband could not afford to leave the state for care.

As she presented herself on MSNBC's Morning Joe, a TV program, one could sense the emotional scars she must bear and the physical pain she described. The fetus was restless and in distress most of the time. Just think of the months of senseless agony she experienced.

Amanda Zurawski has become one of the faces harmed by the abortion laws. She is one of five Texas women suing the state for denying her the right to an abortion and putting her life at risk. Her problem was an "incompetent uterus," which means she could not carry the fetus to term. Her facial expression was flat, affect, depression, and sad.

Recently, these were three bad legal acts. First, the Supreme Court supported the Texas Vigilante Law. This first bad act led to a second bad act, overturning Roe in 2022. The third bad act is the one decided by the "brilliant" judge in Texas, Judge Karsmarcyk, this year, 2023. This one ignores the research and scientists of the FDA to ban the abortion pill Mifepristone.

In Texas, ambiguous laws have crippled doctors and as a result they are having to leave the state. They were tired of looking over their shoulders for fear of losing their licenses or being arrested. In addition, medical schools have reported a sharp decline in applications for OB/GYN.

In Louisiana, Steve Scalise, their U.S. representative stated that overturning Roe was "only the beginning". You may recall that it was in Louisiana that the mother of a headless fetus was denied an abortion and was forced to carry the baby to term.

Most probably some of the "bad acts" would not have occurred if the justices were to function in an ethical environment, because ignorance, arrogance and a lack of ethics have not put us in a respectable place.

CHAPTER ONE

THE OPINION AND THE LEAK

The leak is not the gregious act. It is the opinion that is egregious.

— Professor Laurence Tribe Harvard Law School Cambridge, Massachusetts.

To my surprise and disappointment, Chief Justice of the U.S. Supreme Court, John Roberts, speaking about the leak to overturn Roe, stated that it was "a singular egregious act." I could not disagree more. However, my thinking was later affirmed by someone I respect more in the legal system than anyone else, Professor Laurence Tribe.

As I listened to Lawrence O'Donnel one evening recently on MSNBC's *Last Word,* a T.V. program, Professor Tribe was asked what he thought about John Roberts' statement. Professor Tribe said: "The leak is not the egregious act. It is the opinion that is egregious."

When he said that, I felt a deep sense of pride. Awesome! He took my script!

Professor Tribe went on to cite examples of what he meant by egregious. He included the case of the eleven-year-old girl who was forced to travel from Ohio to Indiana to terminate a pregnancy that was caused by rape. Ohio law did not permit abortion.

There is pause to wonder why Justice Alito wrote such an opinion in the first place. Apparently, Roe was working for America, perfect or not. Besides, the bottom line is that nothing he or anyone else writes or says is going to stop women from having abortions. He is ignorant to believe otherwise. Justice Alito only caused hurt, chaos and confusion.

If Justice Alito had taken the appropriate steps and held discussions and consultations with OB/GYN professionals, it is doubtful that he would have written what he wrote. They would have enlightened him.

The decision to overturn Roe has not only denied women rights but has also prohibited physicians not to practice as usual. The appearance of treating an abortion patient could threaten their own livelihood. Laws vary from state to state and are not clear at best.

Consider the case of the New Orleans married woman who had a spontaneous abortion (miscarriage) that was incomplete and left her bleeding. She went to the emergency room. The staff there hesitated to treat her because of the unclear law. She was sent home with the threat of bleeding to death. What?

Sometimes a fetus is detected on ultrasound to be so badly deformed that viability is not possible outside the uterus. Therefore, abortion is the right and humane thing to do, I believe. We have never encountered a headless human being walking this earth. Well, a mother in Louisiana was forced to carry the fetus to term because of abortion laws.

The deformed embryo and the incomplete abortion are not the only obstetrical problems facing women. Physicians must deal with emergencies such as an ectopic pregnancy. An emergency intervention is required when the embryo has embedded itself in the Fallopian tubes and attempts to grow there where growth is not possible. The only solution is surgery and an abortion. The mother's life is at stake through no fault of her own.

I am not aware of any research or due diligence Justice Alito did to discuss or confer with experts in the field of OB/GYN medicine on the topic of abortion and its many ramifications before issuing his opinion. My gut feeling tells me he did none.

It is interesting, too, about the leak itself. Each and every time I mention it to those familiar with the matter, they invariably reply, "He did it!" referring to Justice

Alito. "He leaked Hobby Lobby, didn't he?" An abortion advocate I am not.

However, I do advocate for women's rights and the rights of physicians to practice freely. I do not believe that Justice Alito has the right to deny our rights just because he could. Shame on him! It was sheer ignorance on his part and that of his colleagues. They were short on facts, information and circumstances. Their fingers were not on the pulse of the people.

The Vigilante law and overturning Roe prompted me to write the following to the newly appointed Supreme Court Justice Ketanji Brown Jackson (in part):

Ketanji Brown Jackson

Shatters the Glass Ceiling!

Many citizens shuttered when seemingly retarded senators

attempted to tarnish her brilliance.

However, her controlled response to them was

grace, tolerance, and resilience.

More importantly, during her stay,

she may help to restore confidence

in the Court that has apparently lost its way,

back to one of morals, integrity, and

a higher level of cognitive functioning.

If achieved, she will surely make our day!

Overturning Roe caused many protests and demonstrations to which Justice Clarence Thomas responded with, "Get over it!" Well, we will get over it when you stop being ignorant and unethical and arrogant.

CHAPTER TWO

GROSS IGNORANCE AND AMERICAN ARROGANCE

He who knows not, and knows that he knows not, is simple. Teach him. He who knows not and knows not he knows not, is a fool! Shun him. He who knows and knows that he knows, is wise. Follow him.

— Author Unknown

Today, abject ignorance and arrogance have resulted in an all-time low of 6% in the confidence level of the Supreme Court. Respect for some of its members dwindled as well. The first blow to the integrity of the Court was majority support and approval of the Texas Vigilante Law. Then, Justice Alito decided that he could become more notorious or famous by writing his opinion to overturn Roe.

The Alito opinion "leaked" which should have provided an indication to a rational person this decision was not going to be well-received. Protest marches occurred through the country.

During this time I wrote to Chief Justice Roberts and pleaded with him not to allow the Alito opinion to become law. While he did not vote with the majority, he did state publicly that the majority members "dug in" after the leak. He submitted the opinion as previously planned.

As a result of overturning Roe, the ramifications have been tremendous. The justices were unable to see the big picture and the chaos that has followed. Sheer ignorance and arrogance have brought us this big mess we have today. The reasons are clear: *First* and foremost, whatever gave Justice Alito the notion that he could end abortions? Abortions have been around for centuries. Nothing he can do or say or write is going to change that. He only puts lives at risk.

Second, I seriously doubt that he can even do a reasonable diagram of the female reproductive system and list the functions of its parts. And he wants to pass a law on abortion?

Third, Roe was not perfect, but it worked for Americans. It was not broken, so he had no need to "fix it".

Fourth, he wrote the opinion not because he thought it was needed, he wrote it because he could! I believe this is as about as low as a human being can go given the significance in the lives of human beings and the untold chaos it has caused. Not only had that he bragged about pulling it off.

Fifth, he usurped the role of the physician to diagnose and treat their patients, especially in emergencies. Sometimes it's a matter of life or death and the doctor finds himself looking over his shoulders to see if the law allows him to do this when time is of the essence.

Sixth, he took away the right of a woman to have control over her own body. I wonder how he would feel when having been forced to have a vasectomy for fathering a child. Some women lose their ability to bear children following untoward prenatal care.

Seventh, maternity wards are closing because the OB/GYN doctors can no longer practice safely in the states such as Texas and Idaho. This causes untold stress on other women who need maternity services.

Eight, no doubt medical students or those considering women's health will think twice, therefore possibly causing a shortage of doctors.

So many women have had their lives put at risk in one way or another because of Justice Alito's opinion. In Louisiana a woman was forced to carry a headless child to term. Five women in Texas sued the state due to a lack of physicians to treat them, forcing an out-of-state trip for an abortion. Others have had spontaneous abortions and miscarriages and were denied care.

While Justice Alito has had no problem putting the lives of women at risk, he complained about his own safety and protection after the opinion. Who cares!

However, within the Supreme Court, Justice Alito comes in second in ignorance and arrogance to Justice Clarence Thomas.

I concur with a recent article written by Erin Aubry Kaplan in the *Los Angeles Times* "Clarence Thomas Earns Our Scorn". She states that, "It's been a long time coming. For most of three decades the ultra-conservative jurist stood in the shadows, on the sidelines, largely silent. He wrote little in the way of opinions and said less. In photos he always looked unhappy and uncomfortable as if acutely aware of what critics thought of him, especially the many Black people [I am number one] who saw him as an entirely unworthy replacement for civil rights hero Thurgood Marshall.

Of course, it was President George H. W. Bush that put Thomas on the Court – but it is Thomas who has long borne the brunt of our scorn. He's earned it!

Now, at last, he commands attention. His concurring opinion in the court decision to overturn Roe v Wade doesn't just concur, it urges the right wing toward more fascism, more undoing of rights not explicitly articulated in the 14th Amendment, and rights Thomas believes are not protected by 'substantive due process.'

To be a Black 'originalist' Supreme Court Judge who believes he must adhere to a document that was designed to exclude and dehumanize people like him is just surreal.

That is not about conservatism, it's about defying reality because you can. It's about indulging in the worst kind of American arrogance. Thomas is making the most of the opportunity." What a shame! He supported Justice Alito's opinion on abortion.

CHAPTER THREE

WOMEN HAVING THEIR SAY: A SURVEY

Look and see which way the wind blows before you commit yourself.

– Aesop's Fables

People have a right to participate in decisions that affect them. Therefore, a survey was conducted by the author using a cross-section of different ages, races and religions. Their point of view was important to me.

Participants were asked to please provide your opinion on the following:

1. Chaos caused by Judge Alito's opinion.
2. Irresponsible Supreme Court.
3. Lack of knowledge about (abortion) and problem pregnancies.
4. The complete absence of male responsibility for the pregnancy.
5. Should decisions about abortions be made by politicians as Dr. Oz suggested?
6. Other comments.

Number 1: Chaos Caused by Justice Alito's Opinion

- "It is time to heed the Constitution and return the issue of abortion to the people's elected representatives." This is a quote from the Supreme Court Justice who with this statement says that those in power determine what can or cannot happen to a woman's body. What would men do if their representatives told them what they can or cannot do to their bodies?
- He made the wrong decision and I question his bases for action.
- Chaos caused by Judge Samuel Alito opinion. As a Supreme Court Judge, Alito should have been aware that his comments about overturning Roe v Wade would cause chaos.
- This, without a doubt, affects poor and people of color disproportionately who are unable to travel to another state to get the abortion.
- I think he made a mistake because he has taken away a personal choice and people will die from illegal abortions.
- Enable conversations about the stories of women who need/seek abortions. Keep the stories in the spotlight and, as appropriate, in our literature and entertainment.
- I could go on and on about this subject, but it makes me furious when someone takes ownership of my own body! Thank you for reading what I think! Hugs.
- You don't go to an artist when you have a question about math! Questions on health require the appropriate doctor. It is insane to think otherwise.
- The fact that Judge Samuel Alito condemned the leak of his (draft) abortion ruling decision was a good indicator of how wrong and unpopular his decision. He is now living in fear for his life.
- The overturning of Roe v Wade has endangered the lives of women.

Number 2: The Irresponsible Supreme Court

- They are not listening to the people. They are making decisions
- according to their personal beliefs.
- Other laws will be overturned like interracial marriages and same sex marriages.
- The Supreme Court only considered the ethics of a textbook view of abortion, rather than considering its social consequences. In other words, it may seem unjust to terminate the viable meaning of sperm plus egg, but it is equally unjust to ignore any health risks the mother may face in carrying the fetus to term or her inability to raise the child.
- Why are we surprised that those five judges took a limited view of the world and deemed theirs's the most desirable?
- Clearly, the judges were not thinking of any of the ramifications of their actions.
- So, all these women who are forced to have children…what legal ramifications are there for the men who got them pregnant? Shouldn't the men have to provide care, education, financial support until the child reaches the age of 18? Sounds like this not only discriminates against women, but even more, women of color and the poor. This will ensure that many women will not achieve financial stability while men are able to strut around carefree.
- Support for pregnant women in areas where abortion care has been restricted.
- Overturning ROE was irresponsible. No consideration was given for the needs of the mother. No thoughts were considered about the ways that abortions were done before abortions became legal.
- Wrong decision for women and the times we live in!
- Overturning Roe was an act of regression which returns the United States to the Dark Ages.

Number 3: A Lack of Knowledge About (Abortion) and Problem Pregnancies

- Lack of knowledge about problem pregnancies clearly the members of the Court have very limited medical background related to abortion, risks and needs of individual women.
- Lack of knowledge about problem pregnancies. The people voting to overturn ROE have no concern about problem pregnancies. They are only interested in their narrow religious beliefs.
- Stop donations and support for anti-abortion political groups and candidates.
- The courts do not have knowledge about problem pregnancies.
- The overturning of Roe versus Wade will result in more women dying without a doubt. If Alito was hoping to preserve life by overturning Roe versus Wade, he failed miserably. In fact, many women who would like to have children, may be hurt the most.

Example: A friend very much wanted to have a child, but her doctor told her that the baby had no heart or lungs. Because of Alito, she and her doctor had to go to court to be able to abort. For three weeks, she became very sick because the body was decaying in her uterus. Finally, the court granted her doctor the right to perform the life-saving abortion.

Example: A friend wanted to start a family, but found out her pregnancy was ectopic. She too had to go to court to get permission to have this pregnancy terminated. In the meantime, her fallopian tube burst and she nearly lost her life.

A woman and her doctor should be able to choose the solution freely to save the former's life. The courts need to keep out of this most personal decision. It's tough enough to choose for yourself, let alone someone else dictating what you can and cannot do; this person is not your doctor, but a politician!

- As stated earlier, the Supreme Court ignored the possible negative ramifications of a child born to a mother that may be incapable of responsibly raising a child, or will have health issues when carrying the pregnancy to term.

Number 4: The Complete Absence of Male Responsibility for the Pregnancy

- Enhance sex education curriculum in our school system.
- How do we evaluate male responsibility for an abortion?

I discussed this in #2 above. I'm sure prominent politicians made sure that their mistresses all received abortions. What a bunch of hypocrites! If abortions are not permitted, then all men must agree to raise their children to the age of 18 or they should be arrested for being a menace to society!

"If men could get pregnant, abortion would be a sacrament." You'd think the patriarchy would get a clue! Aren't any of them married? Don't any of them have daughters? Or maybe that's the whole conspiracy, to preserve the patriarchy and male domination!

- I don't know what they can really do about the men.
- They make some of them pay child support, but many times the ladies do not know who the fathers are. Some men are falsely accused.
- It seems that the Supreme Court Justices and politicians forgot that men are a necessary part of procreation.
- Men taking the responsibility to prevent pregnancy would not cause women to need to consider abortion.
- Need to bring that item to the forefront in news media and TV shows.

Number 5: Should Decisions be made by Politicians such as Dr. Oz?

- Should decisions about abortion be made by politicians as Dr. Oz suggested? No!

  Politicians should not make decisions about abortions. What do they know? (R.N. C.S., Ret.)

- Should decisions about abortion be made by politicians as Dr. Oz suggested: Absolutely not!
- Dr. Oz was pandering to whomever would support him.
- Having a politician determine a life and death matter is ridiculous! the #1 killer of women in the 1800's was childbirth. I get the idea that childbirth may supercede heart attacks in the near future! The year is 2023; I can't believe we've gone so far back! Aren't we supposed to become closer to an egalitarian society? We've made a tremendous leap backwards!
- Should decisions about abortion be made by politicians as Dr. Oz suggested?
- Decisions about abortion should be made by medical people.

Number 6: Other Comments

- How do we address the topic of abortion within our various religions?
- A Survey Response

I was sitting in church the Sunday after Roe v Wade was overturned. Actually, I was biting my tongue as Father was openly gloating over the fact that abortion was not automatically legal in the United States! My husband and I had a hard time sitting through the thirty-minute sermon. Father was so sure that more human lives would be saved and that God had answered all his prayers.

Although I'm a practicing Catholic, I do not think that anyone should force their beliefs upon another person. Let's just say that I am a firm believer in separation between Church and state! So, for me, Father crossed the line. I always felt that the words from the song, *They'll know we are Christians by our love!* Was my mantra; I tried to live by example.

It didn't take long before I realized how wrong Father was. On my morning hike, I greeted one of my fellow hikers who I had not seen for a few weeks. She had been excited about the eminent birth of her first grandchild. Unfortunately, she needed to fly to

Kentucky due to complications with her daughter's pregnancy. Her grandchild had not developed lungs and the doctor recommended an abortion immediately to preserve the mother's life. Here's where things get complicated.

In Kentucky, abortion is illegal. Even though the fetus is legally dead, the daughter was unable to get an abortion without a court order. So, in addition to hearing her child was dead, the mother must appeal to a judge to get permission to terminate her pregnancy. Over the two weeks she waited for the judge's decision, her health deteriorated precariously. Here is someone who wants to give birth, but nearly loses her life because Roe v Wade was overturned.

Another friend whose sister lives in Ohio was up to her eyeballs in this mess!

Ohio bans any abortion after the six week "heartbeat" test of a child's development. It's great if you have a predictable menstrual cycle but it gets dicey if you don't. A pregnancy test confirmed the sister was expecting. She was looking forward to having this child, but on closer examination, it was determined to be an ectopic pregnancy. Normally, this would be an emergency operation, but because of so many misunderstandings in the new law which penalizes the doctor who performs the abortion, a second opinion was sought. This put the patient's life in jeopardy! How does this improve a woman's health?

As far as I can tell, without the support of Roe v Wade, pregnancy/ childbirth may be the number one cause of a woman's death; this was true during the Dark Ages. Although heart disease is currently the number one cause of death for women, this man- made catastrophe could make it fall to the second most dangerous!

Retired Teacher

Conclusion

While I am not surprised by the results of the survey, I am intrigued by those women who had no opinion on anything, as though they could not think, or was afraid to think for themselves. What a shame!

CHAPTER FOUR

WHY PUNISH THE POOR?

Having a baby is harder when you're poor.

*— Catherine R. Pakaluk Asst. Professor,
Catholic Univ. of America*

"Back in the day" when I was growing up in rural Mississippi, there was never any discussion centered on abortion or birth control.

All the women who got pregnant carried the fetus to term, including two teenage cousins. Or, so I thought at the time.

However, it did occur to me that while many of these women had large numbers of children like my mother and her two sisters-in-law, other women had few. Did these women know something the others didn't?

When my mother was asked why she bore so many children, she calmly said, "I could not help myself." So, it was that she just didn't know. I don't recall anything my dad had to say on the topic. He behaved as though it was all normal, and never complained about providing what he could for us.

In today's world we are made aware of those who find it necessary to seek illegal back-alley abortions like California Congresswoman Barbara Lee, or induce at home abortions. Her experience has been reported and repeated countless times. Some of the attempted self-induced abortion produced death in untrained hands. They were not safe. Thus, the need for reproductive centers.

A young neighbor made me aware of a memoir her grandmother had written that included her abortion when she learned that I was writing this book. When she handed me the copy of the memoir, she said, "Privileged".

The abortion took place back in the day in an urban setting worlds away from my mother. The grandmother's mother had given her two pills prescribed by a physician. She expelled the fetal tissue with some difficulty. The process appeared rather routine with the grandmother. How many poor women have the money or the knowledge to seek a doctor's prescription?

The Guttmacher Institute, a research group that studies women seeking abortions, found that seventy-five percent of women were of low income. "More than half already had children and worked in physically demanding jobs with fewer labor protections and less flexibility than higher wage positions."

In a recent *New York Times* International article, "Taking the Abortion Fight to the Street", no men around the country commented about the decision to overturn Roe.

Kim Schultz, 63, Madison Wisconsin:
"It's unbelievable! It's too far of a step backwards. I was stunned and enraged that we could go back in time like this."

Diana Wiener, 82, New York City:
"The court decision will not stop abortion. It will only kill women." She had an abortion in the Bronx in 1959. *"We did not have birth control."*

Michelle Anderson, 52, Dallas, Texas:

"Even before Roe was reversed, Black women had to fight harder to control their own bodies. White women won't do what they should do – they are too afraid to vote against their own privileges."

Tamika Middleton, Madison, Wisconsin:

"Our fight is for full reproductive freedom." She should have the right to choose.

Bruna Monia, 35, New York City:

She cried when she learned Roe was overturned. She said she was concerned for her 18 months old daughter's right to choose.

Kamala Harris, Vice-President of the United States:

"Let us not be tired or discouraged because we are on the right side of history."

Daniel Williams, a historian sums it up this way:

"At some point people will have to recognize that there is no national consensus among those opposed to abortion."

CHAPTER FIVE

DO THE RIGHT THING

Any man can make mistakes, but only an idiot persists in his error.

— *Cicero*

Just imagine the highest court in the land having the need to be reprimanded for misconduct. It is apparently necessary with a six-percent confidence rating.

Senator Chris Murphy has undertaken the effort to introduce legislation to adopt a code of ethics for the Court. One would want to believe that a code already existed. The problem with Senator Murphy's code is that the members of the Court do not have to abide it, nor does it have the apparent ability to monitor or discipline themselves.

Physicians use the Hippocratic Oath to guide their behavior. The essence of which is "Do No Harm". Nurses have long been guided by the Florence Nightingale Pledge which was adapted from the Hippocratic Oath. Nurses have been at the top of RAND's trustworthy list for many years. (Please see appendices for Hippocratic Oath and Nightingale Pledge.)

The Nightingale Pledge reminds me of who I am every day of my life, and who the physician treating me is expected to be. My heart takes an extra beat each time I see it demonstrated.

Overturning Row was as egregious to me as the wrong medication that could have ended my life. I spoke up then. And I am speaking up now.

It was no big secret. I had a problem blood pressure for years. Now it was having an untoward effect on my kidneys. To prevent further damage, better blood pressure regulation was recommended, as hypertension is a primary cause of kidney disease. My private physician suggested a cardiologist at UCLA. He was seen as the wizard on problem blood pressure. It took some time to get an appointment with him. I missed the first one due to knee replacement surgery. But what my surgical team did not know was why I had the appointment with him in the first place. So, they scheduled me to see someone else. The cardiologist was a young thing who did not know his head from his hiney. He told me if I cancelled surgery he would do a work-up. WHAT!!!

Whatever his write-up showed about my visit did not sit well with medical powers that be and he was seriously reprimanded.

Following recovery from the knee surgery, it was time to try for the appointment with the wizard. He still had a full calendar of appointments for some time. Yet, I wanted to see him and only him about my problem.

With two weeks to go, I had my regular three month visit with the nephrologist. It was nothing particularly different about the blood pressure, high but not extremely high that one needed to worry about stroking-out or a heart attack. When she told me she was adjusting the medication, I ask her if I could remain taking what I was already on since I was going to see the cardiologist in two weeks. She behaved as though she never heard a word I said. So, without changing my current medications, she ordered: Nifedipine ER 60 mg Tab 2X per day. I asked her if she had a lower dose.

Again, she behaved as though she did not hear me. Even after I picked up the prescription I tried to question her about taking three BP medications. She did not return my inquiry.

Well, after several days on her medication, along with the previous ones, I became totally incapacitated. There's no doubt in my mind that had I kept taking it, death would have ensued.

Finally, the day of my appointment with the cardiologist came. I told him I could not function on the Nifedipine, and that "winning the battle is useless if you lose the war."

"I get what you mean," he said.

His approach to the problem was very professional. His orders were clear and I felt I was in safe hands that I could trust. At this point I began calling him "Sherlock" after the fictional detective, Sherlock Holmes. As a nurse I considered myself "Watson", his assistant. We would solve the problem together.

On my next visit to the nephrologist, I felt like smoke was coming out of my ears, I was so angry. Someone had driven me to the appointment so I did not want to discuss the problem in her presence. I wrote the following and gave it to her:

The Hippocratic Oath: Do No Harm!

That Nifedipine damn near killed me! I can see why 150,000 – 200,000 people die each year from medications.

1. You had other options.
2. I asked if you had a lower dose.
3. You knew my visit to the cardiologist was coming up.
4. You failed to respond when I tried to reach you. "Dr. Sherlock" agreed with me.

I asked her to read it later when she got the chance. She opted to open it then and there. Her response was without apology. She simply said: "I knew you were going to see him ("Dr. Sherlock").

Well, she got it between the eyes, too, from the powers that be, whose job it is to correct destructive behavior.

Until this day I don't know what possessed her to do what she did. She was aware that I was to see the cardiologist in two weeks. Was it to impress him of her knowledge that she knew how to manage her patients? I do not know. Analogy: until this day I do not comprehend what benefit overturning Roe is to society, as either Justice Alito had the option of leaving the law alone as it was, just the nephrologist and the BP medication. It was apparently working for the majority.

Yet, he ignored the voice of the people following the leak and has yet to apologize for making a mistake. Thousands of women will lose their lives as a result of his opinion and all he cares about is his safety? Desperate people will do desperate things!

Did his ego prompt him to top the Vigilante Law? I wonder, but it seems more like arrogance.

CHAPTER SIX

WHAT DO THESE BRILLIANT MEN DO ABOUT THE MEN?

Politicians have forgotten that men are a necessary part of procreation.

– Katherine Koller, RN

What do the men do about men and abortion? I believe I can answer my own question: nothing – absolutely nothing! Just let them run free with no conscience, no accountability, no sex education and no responsibility. The woman does not get pregnant by herself as we all know, it takes a man!

The brilliance of ignorance is reflected in the lack of any mention of the male's involvement. The survey provided no insight either as to a logical approach. My feedback was better male sex education, and men who take responsibility..

My only new information came from a source in Australia. Men can get an injection that renders them infertile for a two-month period.

Perhaps the "brilliant" Justice Thomas could write an opinion on mandatory vasectomies. Conception begins after ejaculation.

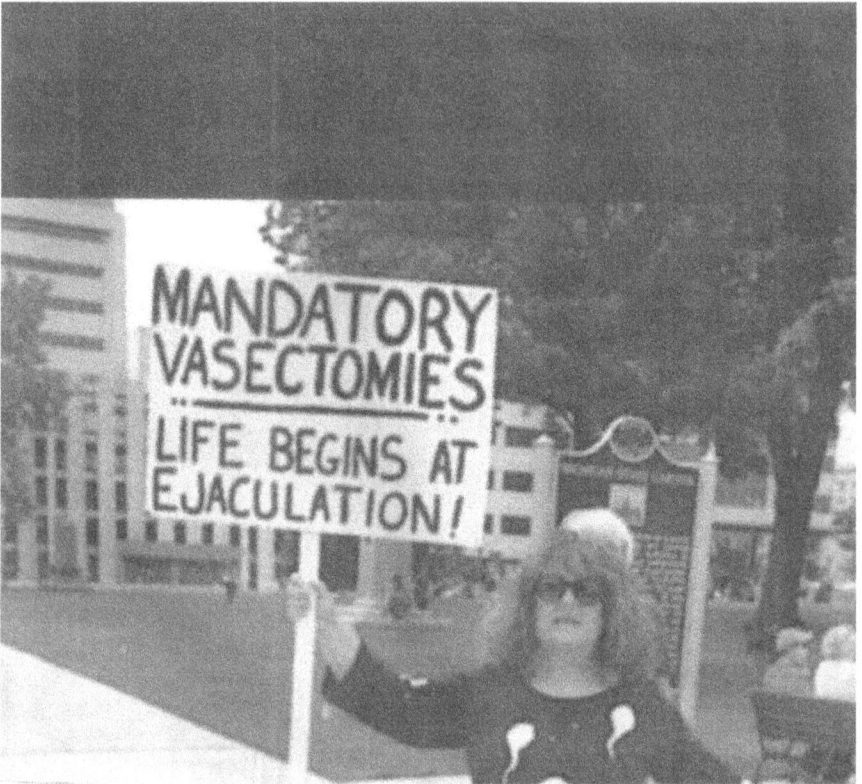

CHAPTER SEVEN

PREVENTING UNWANTED PREGNANCIES

Even with effective affordable, over-the-counter birth control, women will wind up pregnant even though they don't want to be, and in many states forced to give birth against their will.

— Christine Henneberg, M.D.
California Practicing Physician

The good news made my day! I believe my heart skipped a beat with a sigh of relief. The FDA had just announced a new birth control pill that could be sold over-the- counter. The pill, Norgestrel or the Opill will be available to the public within months.

Much of the anxiety surrounding abortion and unwanted pregnancy would now cease, or so I thought at the time. Then I read an article by a practicing physician familiar with the problem. Dr. Henneberg states that the Opill is a "hollow victory because it is only 91% effective. That is nine women in 100 will still become pregnant over a year.

Naturally, I'm disappointed if what she says is true. It means that a woman would still need a Plan B if she becomes pregnant.

According to Dr. Henneberg, "Pregnancy prevention is never perfect, that no contraceptive method is 100% effective," and, "the Opill is not the most reliable means available" She gives that distinction to the etonogestrel implant which requires an in- office insertion procedure.

The implant is placed under the skin of the inner, non-dominant upper arm.

Convenience is apparently strong motivation and prevents the daily hassle of taking the pill. It is just as effective. Insertion of the device is an out-patient procedure and can be removed at any time.

Dr. Henneberg further states that (pregnancy) "prevention is no solution without a backup plan. When we tout easily accessible pregnancy prevention methods but fail to offer legal abortion, we are giving lip service to autonomy while setting women up for failure."

Apparently, the Opill would be 100% effective if humans did not make mistakes while taking it. Users can sometimes forget or fail to take the pill at the same time each day.

It is estimated that 46% of all pregnancies are either unplanned or unwanted. These statistics are not surprising when we consider the unreliability of contraceptive methods, rape, incest and the high rates of teenage pregnancies. The problem, then, in need of a solution is more effective birth control. I can recall my mother saying convincingly, "An ounce of prevention is worth a pound of cure." Of course she was not referring to sex. She made the statement and I made the analogy.

The efficacy or effectiveness of birth control methods fall into four groups:

Group I
Abstinence
No pregnancies, 0/100

Group II

Less than 1/100 women became pregnant in one year:

    A. Implants

    B. Injections

    C. Intrauterine devices

    D. Skin Patch

    E. Vaginal ring with hormones

    F. Condoms

    G. Diaphragms

Group III

10-20/100 women became pregnant in one year.

    A. Spermicide

    B. Withdrawal

    C. No sex during the most fertile days of the cycle.

Group IV

No birth control.

85/100 women became pregnant in one year.

The different measures to help in preventing pregnancy are explained more fully below.

1. Abstinence

Sexual abstinence is the most effective pregnancy prevention method known to man. However, this strategy is difficult to apply for several reasons. One reason is a lack of self-control when sexual urges are present. The male feels he must act to satisfy the urge; voluntary self-denial or abstaining is not an option. Persuasion, wearing-down of the female, talking them into the sex act occurs too frequently. One will remember the ten-year-old Ohio girl who went to Indiana for an abortion.

A second reason abstinence is difficult to apply is drug use. Couples may avoid sex at certain times of the month to avoid pregnancy. However, drug use lowers inhibition and an assault may occur and sometimes does. The third reason abstinence is difficult to apply is helping females avoid circumstances and situations that could lead to an assault.

Abstinence-based education programs empower youth with information they can use to engage in healthy relationships and avoid problem situations. SDS is also a beneficial aspect of abstinence education.

Sexual abstinence education allows parents to participate informally in the education of their children. The advantages and disadvantages of avoiding sex until the right time cam be emphasized and awareness developed. It is recognized here that not all youth have access to a formal sex education program. Therefore, it is incumbent on parents to be ready to teach and support their offspring. Unwanted pregnancies are higher in populations and communities of low socio economic status.

While Abstinence may be a man focus of sex education programs, they tend to include information on effective contraceptive use such as condoms as well as where to find them.

To be sure, abstinence is a choice that is often violated, leading the way to the many unwanted and unintended pregnancies. Rapists in Texas will be punished according to Greg Abbot, the Governor. How does he intend to identify each rapist? How long will it take? It was a hollow promise.

Among the ways people can abstain from sex is (1) the will to do so; (2) setting boundaries; (3) identifying the boundaries of persons around them;

keeping aware of partners not comfortable with abstinence. Boundaries set are guiding principles that act as a reminder of abstinence.

Abstinence is made more difficult in marriage. Sex can make or break a relationship. Clear communication is necessary between partners. As stated previously, drug use can make communications as well as commitment even more difficult. One's cognitive functioning is impacted by drug use. Many pregnancies result from drug use. Women need to be aware as these unwanted and unintended pregnancies contribute to the statistics.

2. Natural Family Planning Methods (NFP)

Natural family planning is a method used by couples that primarily involves the application of fertility awareness information to reduce the risks of pregnancy. According to the literature, the method has gained popularity in the United States but not globally. However, health care professionals are not familiar with the effectiveness of NFP and therefore unable to educate the patient on its proper use. It is suggested that sexually active individuals wanting to use it, should visit a health care professional on how to use it effectively.

Natural family planning has always been included in a full range of options offered to women seeking family planning care. The various methods are numerous and requires attention and understanding:

A. Calendar-based and fertility awareness based methods. A woman is believed to be fertile five days before ovulation and the day of ovulation. Natural family planning method use a combination of methods to help women identify these days.

B. Rhythm method tracks the menstrual cycle in order to identify the days a woman is most likely to become pregnant, and is one of the oldest forms of natural family planning.

The rhythm method is considered the most effective natural family planning method based on the calendar.

A normal menstrual cycle lasts between 28 and 32 days. Ovulation usually happens around day 14. So one would avoid unprotected sex on days 8-19 since that is the time a pregnancy could occur.

C. Basal Body Temperature (BBT)

The woman takes her temperature as soon as she awakens and before she gets out of bed. She is detecting any changes which may indicate fertility.

D. Hormone Tracking.

Levels of hormones in the urine and cervix are measured for changes.

E. Breastfeeding.

Breastfeeding for past-partum women may be used as a contraceptive.

In summary, the use of natural planning methods in the United States is low, approximately 2% for sexually active women 15-44.

3. Contraceptives

Any device or drug serving to prevent pregnancy. Birth control. Contraception can be subdivided into two groups: hormonal (Progestin-only pills, birth control pills, the patch, a shot and ring; non-hormonal contraceptives include the withdrawal method, condoms, copper IUD, tubal ligation and spermicides.

A. Hormonal birth control methods are very effective with a failure rate of 1% when used properly. The composition of hormone contraceptives is progestin and estrogen. Birth control pills suppress ovulation. Along with the pills that are hormone based is the transdermal patch. A woman wears the patch three weeks in a month and the fourth week allows for withdrawal bleeding. The patch is to be avoided in women with clotting problems.

The vaginal ring produced a huge decrease in unwanted pregnancies. The pregnancy risk is having the ring slip for three or more hours before intercourse. It has worldwide use and is considered functional. It protects against STIs.

An injection called Depo-Provera also provides hormonal contraception. It interferes with the sperm fertilizing the ovum and preventing the production of an ovum. The injection is given every three months. Females experiencing anemia and endometriosis are safe using this method according to the Mayo Clinic. A lack of consistently getting the injection every three months puts the female at risk of getting pregnant. Depo-Provera can also delay fertility after not using it for ten months.

Progestin-only pills (POPs) are hormonal contraceptives constituting progestin-only that must be taken daily. There has been increased evidence over the years supporting the efficiency of POPs. The Opill is a member of this group.

4. Non-Hormonal Contraceptives

Non-hormonal contraceptives are much safer and more effective to be used by anyone, even those with health concerns. They do not tamper with the person's natural hormones.

A. Copper IUD

The copper IUD was recommended to me as a safe, effective birth-control measure by my OB/Gynecologist. With two children thirteen months apart, there was not room for argument. It did not matter to my husband.

The IUD has lower health concerns and is easily reversible. It did cause increased bleeding during the cycle.

Apparently, the working principle of the copper IUD is that it alters the copper concentration in the cervix and hinders sperm ability to fertilize the female eggs.

B. Withdrawal Method

This method of birth control always reminds me of the person who was adamant that all the cancer cells were taken when his mother had lung surgery for cancer. "They got it all!" he said. One cannot see the loose cancer cells left behind and one cannot see the sperm cells that escaped before withdrawal. I believe it is an unreliable form of birth control.

The withdrawal method is also known as the pull-out method, involves preventing sperm entering the vagina by pulling out the penis before ejaculation. The sperm must reach the fallopian tube and fertilize the egg for pregnancy to occur. Pregnancy is not possible if the sperm cannot get past the vagina. The risk of pregnancy is high with this method.

One of the problems with the withdrawal method is knowing the exact time to pull-out. The Cleveland Clinic suggests that an experienced spouse is more likely to know when they will ejaculate. However, despite the experience "other factors such as psychological wellness, physical wellness and substance use" could cause incorrect timing for pulling out. Also, before ejaculation, pre-ejaculation is produced and released. Sperm may also be in the pre-ejaculation fluid leading to pregnancy.

C. Sterilization

Female sterilization is considered to be a safe and permanent method used by women who do not wish to have more children. In each case, the tubes (fallopian) are blocked in some way and the ovum cannot travel from the ovary along the fallopian tubes to be fertilized. Women seeking sterilization should get counseling. The procedures of sterilization are complex, permanent and irreversible. Women should understand this to avoid being resentful later.

D. Vasectomy

Vasectomy is also a sterilization procedure except it is used by men who do not intend to have children in the future. It is among the few ways men can participate in pregnancy prevention. It is 99.9% effective and acts by disrupting the normal movement of sperm. The tubes responsible for transporting the sperm to the testicles are cut using a scalpel and afterward closed. Chronic pain is a rare complication following a vasectomy.

E. Condoms

Condoms are known worldwide as a means of contraception. They are found in different sizes, shapes, textures and scents. There are male and female condoms named according to the user. Male condoms are better known. These tube-like rubber (latex) provide a barrier to sperm entering the vaginal canal during sex. Couples are advised to choose condoms that are well-lubricated to avoid leakage and possibly coming off during intercourse. One may also find spermicide-coated condoms on the market now.

Currently, there are also female condoms available. These contraceptives are as effective as the male condoms. They are designed to ease the insertion and removal of the condom in and out of the vagina.
They are made of synthetic and latex rubber as well as polyurethane.

F. Spermicides

Chemicals applied by females before sex that alter the normal movement of sperm to prevent pregnancy are called spermicides. Spermicides occur in various forms as gels, foams and film. They are easily accessible.

Planned Parenthood estimates the effectiveness at about 79% - 86%. Use is suggested alongside other contraceptives.

Lastly, it cannot be over-stated that a solution to the high percentage of unwanted and unintended pregnancies is still needed.

Norgestrel or the Opill will probably go a long way towards that end. However, the problems pregnant women face that require an abortion are going to always be with us. This I regret, and their reproductive rights should not be denied. I am not aware of anyone who takes pride in the abortion of a viable fetus.

CHAPTER EIGHT

STATE ABORTION BANS AND RESTRICTIONS

Women unable to get legal abortions were dying after being injected with disinfectants, over-dosing on a too rapidly administered anesthetic, suffering a perforated uterus that led to blood poisoning. [Pre-Roe in Los Angeles.]

—**Brittny Mejia** *Los Angeles Times*, 5/2/23

The Supreme Court decision left the states with the mandate to legalize or ban abortion. States banning or restricting abortions were bringing about changes so rapidly that I needed a current update. So, I enlisted the help of my research assistant. At the time I was positive that he would return with Texas heading the list of state abortion bans and restrictions.

Well, it has been said that "one cannot know what he/she doesn't know." Oh, boy, did I not know! What I have learned in the process caused my learning curve to soar, and I was very surprised, too.

First on the list was California. What? California? Liberal California? Yes, I began to question the reliability of the search the assistant made. Then I read on. It seems as though California has not always been the enlightened state on abortion that it is now.

Confirming what my research assistant had found was a much extended article by Brittny Mejia in the *Los Angeles Times*, April 2, 2023, "How the LAPD abortion squad went after women and doctors in pre-Roe era." The article reads something like that out of a horror movie, sending chills down my spine! Women were dying and being traumatized, seeking an illegal abortion. It was a thriving business both for those qualified to do abortions and the quacks.

Brittny Mejia writes: "The abortion squad operated for decades before the U.S. Supreme Court decision in 1973 gave women nationwide the legal right to have an abortion.

Some fifty years later the landmark decision fell. The ruling has further inflamed debate in states across the U.S. about how to protect or finally eliminate the ability to have an abortion.

But it underscores the potential role of law enforcement going forward. Some states and other jurisdictions want to empower police and prosecutors to enforce laws against abortion while others are pushing to minimize their role.

In a still unsettled post-Roe world, no one knows for sure what enforcement of abortion laws will look like. But in L.A. in the 1950s and 1960s, offer a hint into at least one possibility."

Immediately following the abortion ban, thirteen states initiated the law. Currently about half of all states have a ban or some restrictions. Some have severe penalties for violations. Abortion bans restrict women's right to reproductive choice, their healthcare, and also their right to privacy, as well as autonomy, equality, freedom from nondiscrimination and inhuman treatment. It is not an insignificant matter.

Women and girls from low socio-economic communities are believed to be the most affected by the bans. Medical personnel are reluctant to conduct the abortion procedure in cases that are or can be considered legal. The fear of being penalized is great. Debates on abortion bans are on-going with advocates trying to top restrictive measures. Most surprising is the attempt to limit the gestational period for having an abortion. Not one of us has had a word from God saying abortions should be banned at six weeks, three months, six months or not at all. Some are better informed about the viability of the fetus than others. It may be helpful here to look at various bans and restrictions in the states. The incident with Senator Tommy Tuberville of Alabama and the military is an exception.

1. Texas

Texas started this whole mess with passage of the Vigilante Law. I believe it is still the most restrictive and egregious of states banning abortions. The message is "just don't have an abortion!" You can't have an abortion in the state and you may not travel outside the state to have one, either.

Anyone who assists in the travel out-of-state is also breaking the law. Fines are assessed at $10,000. Doctors performing abortions can lose licensure and given a $100,000 fine. Thirteen women are currently suing the State of Texas for not being able to receive the care they needed while pregnant. They had various problems, one was pregnant with twins. One twin needed to be aborted, as it was not going to be viable and was affecting the other twin and the life and well-being of the mother.

2. Alabama

Alabama just passed a six-week abortion ban that does not allow exceptions for rape or incest. The law does justify abortion that threatens the life of the mother. The state has one of the most restrictive laws on abortion. It bans abortion after conception on home remedy and procedural abortions. Abortion may not be achieved through telehealth medication.

Termination of pregnancy for an etopic pregnancy or other deadly abnormality does not exist. Like Texas, one who aids in performing an abortion "faces the risk of being prosecuted and jailed for 99 years."

Alabama has not a reason to be proud. Protestors state that banning abortion is not about saving lives but rather the mind to control women's bodies. Alabama has one of the highest poverty rates in the U.S., and every woman is expected to carry their pregnancies to full-term. According to Treisman the states with abortion bans have the highest child poverty rates. The bans affect many women as many suffer financial hardships or

remain in abusive relationships which impacts children's well-being. States like Alabama with abortion bans report low birth weight and low access to maternal care, affecting the mother's and children's safety. These states provide less financial support to families. They make it difficult for women to take time off work, or look for work or access affordable childcare. Abortion bans in Alabama, like Texas, have had huge consequences for society.

3. North Dakota

North Dakota bans abortion with the exceptions of incest and rape. The abortion can only occur within the first six weeks. It, too, is one of the most strict abortion laws in the U.S. North Dakota law does provide for abortion in case of medical emergencies or due to ectopic pregnancies at any stage of pregnancy. North Dakota lacks any abortion clinics. The last ones moved to Minnesota where abortion is legal. The new abortion laws caused conflict between Republicans and Democrats, with Republicans supporting North Dakota as a pro-life state and Democrats stating that women should have the autonomy to make decisions regarding their own bodies (Ahmed, 2023). Physicians in North Dakota make the same argument as physicians elsewhere. Women who have been raped or got pregnant through incest find it unlikely to know they are pregnant at six weeks. However, physicians who violate the law could face prosecution and become charged. The woman seeking an abortion must be provided an active ultrasound and stay for 24 hours before the abortion procedure.

The North Dakota constitution protects its citizens' rights to life and safety. Citizens in North Dakota want their leaders to protect the right to abortion, but the leaders defy the people's will. This refrain is heard over and over throughout these United States! The ban can have a huge effect on many women in the state. Pregnant women unable to access abortion clinics are obligated to carry the fetus to term. As in other states the abortion ban faces legal challenges in North Dakota.

4. Georgia

Georgia bans abortions after six weeks. The law allows abortion for a few exceptions such as rape, incest or the mother's health. The ban emphasizes the beginning of cardiac activity in the embryo. Historically, women have had greater access to reproductive freedom than they see today. Georgia placed more restrictive abortion bans at six weeks, reinstated after the Supreme Court overturned abortion rights for women.

Georgia abortion ban also requires that patients wait 24 hours after consulting with a health provider to obtain an abortion. Parental consent is required for minors in Georgia, unlike other states where abortion is legal. The state also requires that physicians only provide the services, not other healthcare providers. Georgia restricts Medicaid coverage for abortion services except in limited circumstances. Abortion patients are protected in Georgia as the law prohibits obstruction near abortion clinics. Protests are limited around clinics as the law creates zones that protestors cannot access. The abortion ban has led to a decrease in the number of abortions performed. Georgia reported approximately 4,000 abortions per month but has seen the number of abortions reduced by half since the six-week ban went into effect. After the abortion ban, Georgia has registered the highest decline, with an estimated 1,000 fewer abortions. (Hurt, 2023.) Georgia faces high maternal mortality and people of color are at a greater risk due to pregnancy related complications. The ban on abortion at six weeks has a devastating effect on OB/GYN practitioners as they fear being criminalized for their actions.

5. New Jersey

Abortion in New Jersey currently has no gestational limit. The people of New Jersey were guaranteed the right to terminate or keep their pregnancy. The bill was signed into law by Governor Phil in 2022. The law also prohibits law enforcement cooperation with other states to investigate individuals seeking abortion in New Jersey. Patients have the right to undergo medical or procedural abortion care based on what is best for them. The state also allows for the medication prescription of abortion through telehealth.

Minors are legally protected and can seek abortion services without parental consent.

Providers of abortion services in New Jersey must also comply with some regulations. Abortions performed after 14 weeks must be done in a licensed hospital. Those abortions performed after 18 weeks in a facility where surgical services are nearby. People from other states are allowed to seek abortions in these facilities. However, not everyone in New Jersey is able to access abortion services due to inequality in access to the services. Barriers due to the cost assessing care and a lack of nearby providers can render the service unreachable for many people. New Jersey does have the New Jersey

Family Care that covers abortion with no out-of-pocket costs. The state has minimal regulations for patients and providers seeking abortion services.

6. California

We turn our attention to California again. Abortion in California is legal but limits abortion until the fetus becomes viable. Women can access abortion up to the time that the fetus becomes viable. Pregnant women in the state do not have to provide any viable reason for abortion based on state law. Again, this is possible and allowed before the fetus becomes viable. This is when medical personnel judge that a fetus can stay alive independently. In the second trimester when the fetus can live independently, viable, abortion can only be performed in case of risk to the mother's health. Only qualified medical personnel with valid licenses can perform abortion procedures. Abortions can be done by licensed nurses, nurse midwives and physician's assistants. In the first trimester, abortion is conducted mainly through pill admission. In the second trimester, abortion can be done using surgical instruments. In the third trimester abortion is considered mainly if the mother's life is at risk as the fetus is already viable. Under-age girls have the same rights as adults and can seek an abortion. It is considered unconstitutional to seek parental consent when they require abortion.

California allows people to travel from outside the state to seek an abortion. The practice is commonly called medical tourism. According to a study by the Smith Group (2022) many people traveled to California seeking an abortion, and approximately 15% of all abortions performed in the U.S. are done in California. The environment in California is deemed conducive or very supportive. California does not prosecute persons seeking an abortion nor does the state corroborate with other states' law enforcement offers seeking to prosecute a person for having an abortion in California. Officials from Texas come readily to mind trying to catch someone who escaped their snare to have an abortion. Today, California has one of the most unrestrictive laws concerning abortion rights and supports women's reproductive health. It is a far cry away from the actions of the 1950s and 1960s in Los Angeles.

Different states in the U.S. have different abortion rights, with some states legalizing abortions and others having more strict measures on abortion. State bans affect women's health and especially low economic status women. California is one of the more liberal abortion states but limits are enforced when the fetus reaches viability. Women do not have to provide a reason to seek an abortion. The state is credited with providing approximately 15% of all abortions in the U.S. New Jersey also legalizes abortion and can access abortion care at any stage of pregnancy. Georgia bans abortion after six weeks. In Alabama abortion is banned, without exception, for rape or incest. It is only available when the woman's life is at risk during pregnancy. North Dakota also bans abortion but provides an exception for rape and incest until the sixth week. Different states have different measures concerning abortion, with some being more or less restrictive than others.

CHAPTER NINE

THE UNITED STATES MORALITY POLICE

Women (everywhere) just want to be free.

– Dr. Jill Biden, First Lady Presenter 2023
Emmy Awards

What intrinsic value could ever be derived from forcing women to be second-class citizens? First, they were too dumb to vote; then, they could not have a credit card in their own name. Now, the men have decided they do not have the right to make decisions about their own bodies. We behave like some Third World Country.

It seems as though everyone wearing a pair of britches has an opinion about abortion and what to do about it. Take Senator Lindsey Graham, stating that 15 weeks should be the length of time for a national abortion law. Pray tell me, what the hell does he know about a safe abortion? Then, there is Dr. Oz who should know better, saying the abortion should be decided by the l-o-c-a-l p-o-l-i-t-i-c-i-a-n, the patient and the doctor. This sick thinking should never hit the air waves.

Some examples of women worldwide being denied their rights include a *60 Minutes* segment about high school girls studying in the African country of Rwanda. They were transported there from Afghanistan because the Taliban does not allow girls to go to school. How stupid!

Then we find the women revolting in Iran. The Morality Police do not want them going without their headscarf to keep the hair covered. Some men have been executed because they supported the protest.

In the U.S. the shallow-mindedness is led by Justice Samuel Alito and his posse, the four members who supported his opinion. Greg Abbot, Governor of Texas, and the author of the Vigilante Law that severely restricts abortions in Texas and some GOP politicians.

In addition, there are the many state attorney generals who seek to deny women their rights and who filed suit with a federal judge to ban the abortion pill, mifepristone.

CHAPTER TEN

A STATE OF FLUX AND UTTER CONFUSION

The problem with abortion is the men don't know what to do with the women.

– Michael Steele, Former GOP chairperson

We continually see the profound consequences caused by Justice Alito overturning Roe. This would-be genius, with no medical background, let the genie out of the bottle and now cannot control the fallout or ignorance of politicians.

It is difficult to follow all the various issues surrounding abortion. Court decisions at lower levels are in conflict with each other. Judges are making unsound decisions, i.e. Judge Matthew Kacsmaryk in Amarillo, Texas with the drug mifepristone. Politicians giving their opinions on when to limit the ban. Every GOP lawmaker has something to say about it. There is no ending.

The FDA and pharmaceutical companies must now defend what their researchers and scientists have demonstrated what is obviously a sound and safe medication. How dare he!

Problem issues for women surrounding abortion generally fall in four categories: Access appears to be primary. Most facilities providing care have closed in states where abortion is illegal. Other states do not want the medication delivered by mail or over-the- counter, or prescribed by a doctor.

Legality is a second area of concern. What abortions can be performed without being criminally liable? Is a spontaneous abortion or miscarriage treated differently than a regular abortion?

A third area of concern is when the ban is in effect. Again, every politician with britches on has proposed some sort of ban. Some propose a six-week ban. Others have suggested nine weeks or even fifteen. Imagine Senator Lindsey Graham making such a decision for you, or Governor Ron De Santis of Florida. I think not.

The fourth category of concern is the freedom to travel. In Texas and Idaho it is illegal to assist a person to go out-of-state to seek an abortion. Just think if a woman has an ectopic pregnancy in Texas or Idaho, she will have to appear before a judge to terminate a pregnancy that will never result in a living human being. This is a serious matter and time is of the essence as it could cause her the loss of her fallopian tube or even death.

It appears as though politicians jumped at the chance to make women's power over their own bodies more narrowly constrained after Roe was overturned. Likewise, judges have taken a limited view of the world and deemed that their view is the most desirable. I don't agree!

CHAPTER ELEVEN

A LACK OF ETHICS

Congress can't regulate the Supreme Court.

– Samuel J. Alito Supreme Court Justice

"Congress should come up with a code of ethics for the Court," a retired judge, J. Michael Lattig, stated. However, when Senator Durbin invited Chief Justice John Roberts to discuss the process, he responded that the Court was independent and declined the invitation. "The claim of judicial independence is just a smack in the face," stated Attorney Jamille Bovie. "The Court's legitimacy is everything," says Milissa Murray, Professor of Law.

"Legitimacy" is apparent in terms of our last two Supreme Court Justices' Senate confirmation hearings. Both Justices Cavanaugh and Barrett agreed that Roe vs Wade was "settled law." However, when the Dobbs draft was presented to them, they voted to overturn the law as though they lacked the honesty or truthfulness to admit a proclivity toward the opposite. Was there a hidden agenda all along? The point here is that the decision would not have passed because Justice Alito would not have had the votes without them.

After what Nicole Wallace of MSNBC called a "Boo-Hoo" interview of Justice Alito by the *Wall Street Journal*, it was apparent that Alito is still not feeling accountable for all the chaos and suffering. Senator Sheldon Whitehouse referred to him as "a very angry man!"

At a recent currents events discussion among a large group of members belonging to the silent generation, a lively topic was suggested; "A Code of Ethics for the Supreme Court." While the serious nature of the matter was evident, a non-participant observer would probably chuckle, being reminded of the childhood story, "Who Will Bell the Cat?" You may recall that the rats/mice knew the cat was a problem, so putting a bell on the cat would allow for their safety and well-being. But, WHO was going to put the bell on the cat?

Everyone recognized that the Court needs a Code of Ethics, but how does one solve the problem since the Court itself does not want one; the Senate apparently does not have the authority to create one; and the Court does not have the insight to fix itself; or does the present situation extend into infinity?

Along with the surprise that an important body of professionals like the justices would not have some standards or code of conduct and moral judgment, they proceeded to propose questions. "What do they say when they take the oath of office?" "My wife and I had to take a course in ethics before we could serve on the city advisory board."

"Maybe the Constitution needs to be amended," etc. "Term limits" was suggested, too.

In addition to overturning Roe, another unethical decision that members of the group pointed out was the effect of "Gerrymandering" on voting rights.

The leader of this current events discussion strongly encouraged everyone to see a *Frontline* presentation on Clarence and Ginni Thomas.

He said that we would see what a "flawed man" he is. The fact that he is a Supreme Court Justice is the very essence of unethical.

Since the problem of an unethical Court cannot be solved by the Court itself, we need another mindset. As Dr. Wayne Dyer suggests: you cannot solve a problem with the same mindset that created it.

HE SAID:

- I only wish Nino (the late Justice Antonin Scalia) were here to enlighten us. I would take that evaluation in good humor and learn from the exchange.
- I personally have a pretty good idea who is responsible (for the leak). It was part of an effort to prevent the Dobbs draft . . . from becoming the decision of the Court. And that's how it was used for those six weeks by people on the outside – as part of the campaign to try to intimidate the Court.
- It was rational for people to believe that they might be able to stop the decision in Dobbs by killing one of us (the Court majority).

- I don't feel physically unsafe, because we now have a lot of protection, driven around in basically a tank and I'm not really supposed to go anyplace by myself without the tank and members of the police force.
- . . . This type of concerted attack on the Court and individual justices (is) new during my lifetime.... We are hammered daily and I think quite unfairly in a lot of instances. And nobody, practically nobody is defending us.

On the "shadow docket," "a term coined to refer to applications for emergency orders and summary decisions which the justices handle quickly and without full briefing" – he said:
- They're very disruptive. But what are we supposed to do? They are brought to us.

The last administration brought a lot of them to us because a lot of its programs were enjoined. This administration is doing the same thing right now. The solicitor general has said that she's likely to file application here to stay the Fifth Circuit's order in the case involving the mifesti prone? However you pronounce the word (the drug is mifepristone, an abortion drug).
- I have to prepare for a sitting next week. The next two weeks we have arguments.

I have to prepare for all those cases. But when this comes in, I am going to have to put all that aside and deal with it.

The shadow docket application to stay the Fifth Circuit ruling on mifepristone came to Justice Alito in his capacity as circuit justice on April 14. After issuing an immediate stay, the full Court granted the stay on April 21 pending further litigation.

"Justice Alito filed a written dissent from the order granting the stay."

CHAPTER TWELVE

SENATE PREPARES FOR CODE OF ETHICS FOR COURT

Questions about ethics aren't the only or even the principal reason for dissatisfaction with the Supreme Court.

—**Editorial Opinion** *Los Angeles Times*
July 20, 2023

The principal reason for dissatisfaction with the Supreme Court is not the scandals of Clarence Thomas and Samuel Alito's lavish gift-taking and free travel, it is the over- turning of Roe vs Wade. The Court is very far out of step with public opinion.

It is inexplicable how one can be convinced that accepting lavish gifts and trips can ethically and morally equate or supersede human rights and needs.

Each time ethics is mentioned, it is about the personal conduct of Clarence Thomas' and Samuel Alito's failure to disclose their "takes".

The long-running General Social Survey conducted by the University of Chicago found a 50-year low in trust for the court following the overturn of Roe. Confidence slipped even among Republicans Protests following the leak and the opinions, news media coverage, articles, editorial opinions – all point to the fact that overturning Roe caused an earthquake. Facts also suggest that Alito changed the interpretation of the abortion law simply because he could. Is it not surprising then, that informed people would be upset?

Never in the history of the U.S. has there been the need for barricades and a fence around the Supreme Court building to protect it from siege and protect Justice Alito because of Roe. He also needed personal protection and traveled by "tank". He was advised not to make a speech to law students at a local university because of the fear for his safety.

The Court has lost its way in spite of the denials. Poor decisions have been made before such as those on Gerrymandering and voting rights. However, with little more than a year's time, the Court has overturned two decisions that had precedent, Roe and Affirmative Action and a really dumb Web Design decision on a case that was without an actual defendant.

There is a lack of consideration for precedent as though the importance or reason for its passing in the first place does not matter. Some justices' behavior remind me of growing up in the South, watching vultures wait in nearby trees to devour the carcass of a beloved farm animal.

An AP poll reported "large majorities of Americans said they think a woman should be able to have an abortion if her own health is at risk, if there is a strong chance of a serious defect in the baby or the pregnancy is the result of rape." Justice Alito went to the Constitution to justify not being able to find explicit instructions on abortion law.

What? Then, he said he relied on some ancient law that outlawed abortion. Can you believe this level of thinking during modern times?

A year after the Court stated there is no constitutional right to abortion, it undid the Affirmative Action in college admissions. This was a long-standing law to make attempts to remedy the effects of slavery. The opinion was written by John Roberts.

Writing for the majority, said, "That admissions programs lack sufficiently focused and measurable objectives warranting the use of race, unavoidably employ race in a negative manner, involve racial stereotyping and lack meaningful end points." In understandable English, the American dream has come and gone.

The third decision, poorly conceived, was an opinion written by Neil Gorsuch: The suit had been brought by Lorie Smith, a web designer who said her right to free speech was being violated doing web designs for LGBTQ people. There was no defendant involved in the suit. And to think Samuel Alito bitterly complained when he needed to use his time on the docket case for mifepristone, the abortion drug.

Congress has the power to over-ride Supreme Court rulings. "The prevailing criticisms miss half the problem. The Court's over-reach is a direct result of Congress' under-reach. . .the Constitution requires strong institutions vying against one another to prevent the concentration and abuse of power. . .the justices struck down constitutional precedents such as abortion rights, that the legislature failed to codify and [Affirmative Action] . . .Only Congress can claw back policy making power from the Supreme Court."

The above quote is written by Francesca Procaccini and Nikolas Guggenberger in an article, "Angry About the Supreme Court? Blame Congress."

Senator Sheldon Whitehouse heads the Judiciary Committee to work towards a code of ethics for the Supreme Court. The Court has been given ninety days to indicate progress towards developing their own code. If not, the Senate Ethics Committee will begin work on one.

In a letter to the editor, Jack Quirk responded to Samuel Alito's remark implying that critics of the Supreme Court are motivated by displeasure with recent rulings.

He said:

"I am surely not the first person to identify two distinct points underlying the distrust of the Supreme Court – and at this time, three specific justices.

The issuance of fundamentally flawed decisions in mean- spirited opinions is a matter of judicial malfeasance. On the other hand, an overwhelming indifference to the ethical and moral standards expected to apply to all persons – and particularly to judges – goes to something more fundamental than the absence of consistent principles in the Court's decisions.

I believe both judicial and ethical lapses by this court share a common root– the indifference of specific justices to any standard or principle beyond their own interest and preferences. This lies at the heart of the problem and, on both counts, it disqualifies the justices in question from positions on the Court."

—*Jack **Quirk** Porter Ranch*

Thank you Mr. Quirk! You took the words right out of my mouth!

CHAPTER THIRTEEN

RULES ARE FOR THEE, NOT FOR ME!

Life's most persistent and urgent question is: What are we doing for others?

– Dr. Martin Luther King, Jr.

Reverence for the Supreme Court is shattered; confidence in the Court is at an all- time low. The integrity of the Court is not apparent and ethics went out the window. Yet, Justice Alito is complaining about the amount of criticism the Court is getting with no one defending them.

The rights of ordinary citizens to question those in authority was affirmed by President Biden during his speech at this year's Correspondents' Dinner. "Those in authority" means him and everybody else.

"Rules are for thee, not for me" is communicated everyday by members of the Court. First we heard about Justice Thomas's shadowy dealings with the Texas billionaire; then Justice Gorsuch's non-disclosures of property sales; then the wife of the Chief Justice Roberts' wife's earnings from law firms; Ginny Thomas' participation in the January 6 riots.

While most of the above reporting has to do with cheating the IRS and therefore the American people, Justice Alito's acts are more egregious because they deal with undue human suffering, chaos and confusion. He is too detached from what he's done to see it. He's making laws for the lives and well-being of humans.

First, he supported the dumb law in Texas, the Vigilante Law. His opinion caused the overturning of Roe v. Wade. Now he has just voted against extending the aborting medication Mifepristone, while it works legal arguments through the courts. He still just doesn't get it!

Senator Dick Durbin of the Senate Judiciary Committee extended an invitation to Chief Justice John Roberts to a public hearing to testify on ways to restore the Court's

ethical standards saying that current standards are "inadequate". The invitation was declined. A letter signed by all nine justices indicated that they were policing their own ethics, essentially and Congress does not have the authority to interfere.

In the Appendices are copies of the Hippocratic Oath that physicians follow and the Nightingale Pledge which nurses take upon graduation to guide ethical behavior. The nurses' pledge was adopted from the Hippocratic Oath. Perhaps the Justices can get some guidance from the two of these. They need help.

CONCLUSIONS

Thank goodness! A reporter finally said out loud what has been my thinking all along: "He's in the wrong business" if he thinks he can escape public criticism. The reporter was in a discussion about an interview Justice Alito did with the *Wall Street Journal.* His comments came on MSNBC, Friday, April 28, 2023 during *The Alex Wagner* show. In the interview Justice Alito also expressed his annoyance at having to take time to deal with the Mifepristone issue and the pronunciation of "Mifepristone".

Again, there is nothing that justifies overturning Roe. The law,, perfect or not, was working for America. If it were broken, he sure did not fix it!

However, I do not anticipate that when the issue of Mifepristone comes back to the Court for passage, the other Justices will allow themselves to be led down a "rabbit

hole" again. Of course that does not include Justice Clarence Thomas. We will see if I'm right.

APPENDICES

APPENDIX A

A Letter in Support of a Code of Ethics

Senator Richard Durbin Chair
Senate Judiciary Committee, Hart Bldg. Constitution Avenue and Second St. NE Washington, D.C. 20510

June 4, 2023

Dear Senator Durbin:

It is a pleasure to write to you, one of my very favorite senators, about the topic of a Supreme Court Code of Ethics.

I believe, as I have read that you do, that "the highest Court in the land should not have the lowest standards."

My reverence for the Court is gone and I have lost respect for some of its members. Many of the people I know feel the same way. Confidence is very low.

J. Michael Luttig, a retired judge, stated that "The Congress should come up with a Code of Ethics for the Court." I know you invited Chief Justice Roberts to start the process and he declined, citing Court independence.

May I suggest that you proceed without him? Your legal scholar on your committee could well be led by Professor Laurence Tribe at Harvard, someone who has impeccable integrity, knowledge of the laws and is very much in touch with people. You could seek citizens' drafts as well.

Senator Durbin, *the Court cannot fix itself.* You may take that to the bank. With a mindset like that of Justice Thomas, a very "flawed" individual, and Alito, how could they? Change will be difficult for them.

A course in ethics before senate confirmation seems like an appropriate requirement, too.

Cordially,

Dorris S. Woods, PhD (RN, Clinical Nurse Specialist, Ret.)

P.S. Since you are probably not going to be able to change ethical behavior on the Court, term limits of 12-20 years have been suggested.

cc: Professor Laurence Tribe Chief Justice John Roberts

APPENDIX B

Hippocratic Oath

I swear to fulfill, to the best of my ability and judgment, this covenant:

I will respect the hard-won scientific gains of those physicians in whose steps I walk, and gladly share such knowledge as is mine with those who are to follow.

I will apply, for the benefit of the sick, all measures [that] are required, avoiding those twin traps of overtreatment and therapeutic nihilism.

I will remember that there is art to medicine as well as science, and that warmth, sympathy, and understanding may outweigh the surgeon's knife or the chemist's drug.

I will not be ashamed to say "I know not", nor will I fail to call in my colleagues when the skills of another are needed for a patient's recovery.

I will respect the privacy of my patients, for their problems are not disclosed to me that the world may know. Most especially must I tread with care in matters of life and death. If it is given me to save a life and save life wherever possible within reason; this awesome responsibility must be faced with great humbleness and awareness of my own frailty. Above all, I must not play at God.

I will remember that I do not treat a fever chart, a cancerous growth, but a sick human being, whose illness may affect the person's family and economic stability. My responsibility includes these related problems, if I am to care adequately for the sick.

I will prevent disease whenever I can, for prevention is preferable to cure.

I will remember that I remain a member of society, with special obligations to all my fellow human beings, those sound of mind and body as well as the infirm.

If I do not violate this oath, may I enjoy life and art, respected while I live and remembered with affection thereafter. May I always act so as to preserve the finest traditions of my calling and may I long experience the joy of healing those who seek my help.

APPENDIX C

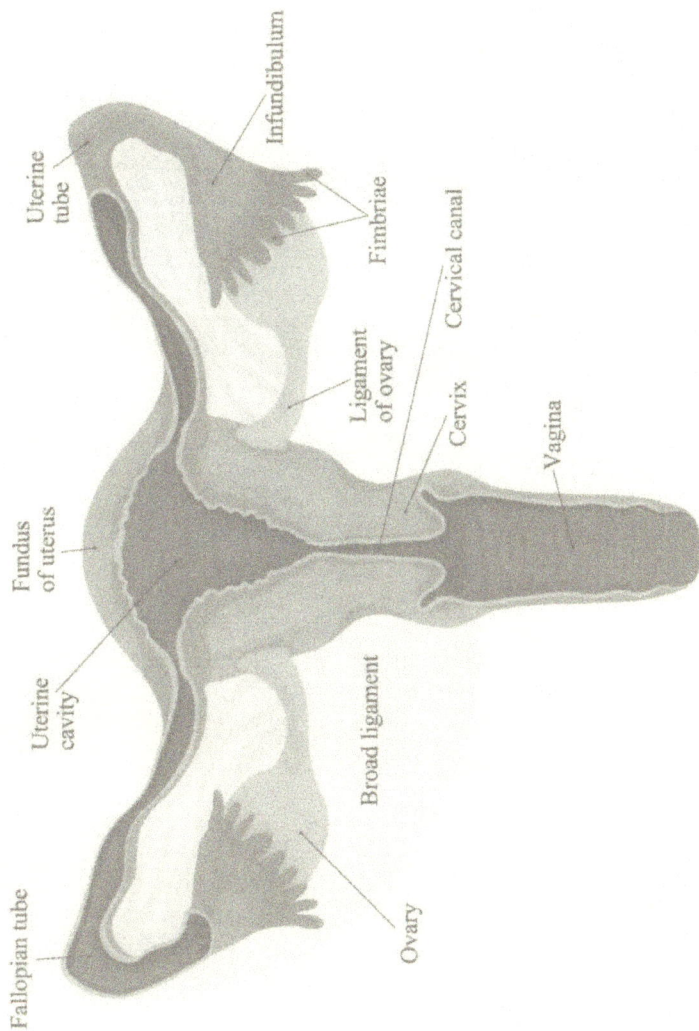

FEMALE REPRODUCTIVE SYSTEM

Fallopian tube

Uterine cavity

Fundus of uterus

Uterine tube

Infundibulum

Fimbriae

Ligament of ovary

Cervix

Cervical canal

Vagina

Broad ligament

Ovary

APPENDIX D

GLOSSARY OF TERMS USED IN ABORTION

- *Abortion* is defined as the expulsion of the product of conception before viability that is before the twenty-eighth week of gestation.
- *Threatened abortion* is one where there is some vaginal bleeding and usually menstrual cramps or backache. If treated early the symptoms may subside.
- *Inevitable abortion* is one where the bleeding and cramps have persisted and there is some dilation of the cervix uteri. Termination cannot be prevented.
- *Incomplete abortion.* One where part of the products of conception is retained in the uterus and bleeding persists.
- *Complete abortion.* One where the entire product of conception is expelled.
- *Missed abortion.* One where the fetus dies and is not expelled but is retained for some time.
- *Habitual Abortion.* Indicates a condition where a patient has several abortions about the same time in succeeding pregnancies.
- *Therapeutic Abortion.* One where pregnancy is terminated legally by a physician, after consultation with other physicians, because it is believed continuation would endanger the life of the mother.
- *Criminal Abortion.* One where the pregnancy is terminated by illegal interference.
- *Pregnancy* is the condition of being with child.

- *Abdominal pregnancy* is the implantation of the ovum (egg) in the abdominal cavity and is not life-sustaining.
- *Ectopic or extra uterine pregnancy* is the growing of the ovum outside the uterus and is not life-sustaining.
- *Embryo:* The term given to the product of conception during the first three months of pregnancy.
- *Fetus:* the term given to the embryo after the end of the third month of pregnancy. The stage of viability.
- *Fertilization:* impregnation of the ovum by the male sperm cell.
- *Ovum:* the female reproductive cell which after fertilization develops into a new member of the same species. The human ovum is a round cell about 1/120 inch in diameter.
- *Sperm cell:* a mature male germ cell, the specific output of the testes.
- *Viability:* the ability to live, grow and develop.

APPENDIX E

BACK STORY ON ABORTION

Abortion is one of the contentious issues within the American context. This is an ongoing debate concerning the justification or rejection of the development of abortion rights among Americans. Different groups have divergent opinions concerning abortion and the legalization of abortion. In American society, the issue of abortion has a historical context and people debate and question the morality of adopting abortion. Some people are concerned with the moral status of adopting the use of abortion (Warren, 2017).

Abortion is understood as the Act of which the woman voluntarily terminates her pregnancy or allows another person to terminate the pregnancy. In all the arguments, what takes precedence is the issue of a woman's right versus the right to protect the unborn

child's life. However, those supporting abortion often indicated that the woman has the right to decide. This paper aims to evaluate the different issues related to abortion. Some of the issues addressed in the paper include the historical background of abortion, the anti-abortion campaign movements and the various political viewpoints in the American context.

Historical Background of Abortion

American society has struggled to develop the right regulations related to abortion, even in the current times. The controversy of abortion continues to exist and has acquired higher-level attention among the different people in society, courts, legislatures and the people of the religion. Therefore, having a historical understanding of the issue is essential. It helps to evaluate the American attitudes over time towards abortion and the key issues related to abortion among the people. Based on evaluation in the 1880s, the issue of abortion was not a critical subject among the people in American society. At the time, the issue of abortion was only practiced in a limited manner by married women (Sauer, 1974). Historical data indicates that the average American family consisted of an average of eight children. Based on the evaluation, in the lifetime of the American woman, they gave birth to an average of seven children indicating that they did not have an abortion and among the married women, they did not seek abortion services. At the time, the stigma that followed abortion made people not to acquire an abortion. However, some non-married women often utilized these services (Sauer, 1974). During the time, abortion was a rare occurrence and most people preferred to remain silent about the issue.

Based on the evaluation, the issue of abortion within American society started way back; however, it was not widespread. Evidence indicates that American society has practiced abortion using different techniques which are specific to communities. At the time, women with unwanted pregnancies adopted different methods of abortion. Based on the evaluation, even before colonization, some of American women knew the use of different herbal medications and other physical methods to help in inducing abortion.

This was common among women in Northern America (Acevedo, 1979). For example, the Indians adopted the use of the black root and the red cedar, which effectively induced abortion among those seeking to abort. During the colonial period, abortion in America was not illegal. At the time, Great Britain did not treat abortion as a crime. However,, they were developed in 1837, when light penalties for abortions were developed (Acevedo, 1979). The first legislation prohibiting abortion was developed in 1821. Over time, the different states initiated their legislation objecting to abortion by the 1830s.

However, there were still ambiguities and controversies related to the developed laws regulating abortions in America.

According to Sauer, 1974, as the number of children grew, the American women became aware of the issue and developed fertility attitudes. Also, there was a general understanding that many children were a burden. Between 1820 to 1900, there was a shift to those attitudes and a decline in the population. The topic of abortion has become a common issue in the public domain. By 1946, more American women were acquiring abortions and by 1859, abortion was one of the prevalent problems in American society. From 1860 to 1870, abortion was a serious issue and was at its peak. After the American civil way, it is reported that in New York only, there were more than 400 abortions. A higher number of advertisements related to people offering to procure abortion (Sauer, 1974). By 1891, numerous people were offering painless abortion remedies to American women.

Beckman (2017) asserts that American states had different regulations related to controlling abortion. Historically, the different states had differing laws regulating abortion before the development of the land market ruling in 1973. Some states had different regulations, and some indicated that a woman has the right to abort the child in the first trimester (Beckman, 2017). In this case, any woman who wished to abort the child had the right to abort, irrespective of the circumstances. In some states, abortion was allowed under certain conditions, including rape cases, when the pregnancy threatened the pregnant woman and in cases of incest. In most states in America, abortion was illegal.

The development of the landmark ruling in 1973 helped reduce the ambiguity of abortion laws.

Reasons for Roe v Wade

Roe v. Wade's ruling in 1973 helped in solving the challenges related to the regulation on abortion rights among the people. One of the critical reasons issued by the judge is that women have the right to privacy under the constitution. In this case, the American constitution gives them the right to decide on securing an abortion. Therefore, based on the evaluation of the ruling, it supported the legalization of abortion among women in their first trimester in all states (Beckman, 2017). Before the landmark ruling, only a few states had adopted laws supporting abortion among women in their trimesters.

In the determination of the court ruling Roe v. Wade indicated that the 14th Amendment provides privacy of all people. In this case, the concept of personal liberty must be upheld and in this case, the women have the right to decide on their pregnancy. The court also resonated that the American constitution did not evaluate and outline what it meant to have the right to privacy (Linton, 1989). However, the court resonated that only personal rights may be understood as fundamental or mean an implicit concept of ordered liberty. These are the critical issues that help guarantee the individual right to privacy. The court further justified abortion as a fundamental right by re-evaluating English and American law. During the evaluation, the court decided that the common law, due to the adoption of the American constitution and in the 19th century, abortion was widely accepted (Linton, 1989). The majority of women enjoy the right to terminate their pregnancy in the majority of the states at the moment. In the 19th century, women had the right to keep or terminate their pregnancy, especially during the first stages. Even with the evaluation of the law, there were no severe cases of punishment among the women who procured abortions.

The Anti-abortion Movement

The court ruling on the Roe v. Wade decision and the recognition of the constitutional right to engage in abortion generated the discourse about the women's freedom and bodily autonomy. The decision resulted to division among the people in society as some objected to the idea that women should have the legal right to abort (Weitz, 2010). At the same time, there was the development of the slogans such as "abortion on demand" and "abortion without apology" that supported engagement in abortion. It was perceived as the awakening of modern feminism in American society. During the period around 1970, there was a growing group of people who objected to the ideals related to abortion. People objected to the idea of abortion and engaged together to form the anti-abortion movement. As a result, political action committees were developed to support and elect candidates who were against abortion rights. As a result of this mass action, Ronald Reagan was elected as the president who was pro-life (Weitz, 2010). In this case, the election of President Reagan aimed at ensuring that he included the development of anti-abortion polices and an agenda. Adopting the abortion right gained momentum; the anti-abortion movement also dramatically increased its societal initiatives. Fried (2013) indicates that the pro-abortion activities thought that the issue of abortion is settled and now they devoted their resources to ensuring that these services were made affordable and easily accessible among the women who exercised their rights. However, there was the emergence of anti-abortionist groups at the national level with their vision of conservatives and an end to abortion rights. These people engage in the struggle to change the legal status of abortion in the larger culture war and the social meaning of abortion. The anti-abortion movement engages in activities of changing the heart and the understanding of Americans to reject the adoption of abortion policies. They aimed at ensuring that the practice of abortion was made unworthy and that society should not approve the utilization of these new regulations as part of protecting the lives of unborn children.

The anti-abortion movement engaged in different activities that aimed at overcoming the challenge of abortion. They adopted a multidimensional by utilizing images related to the fetus and helping people understand the negative issues related to abortion. The group shared different types of images concerning the abortion procedure that aimed at making people aware of the ills of engaging in abortion (Weitz, 2010).

These groups also engage in targeting the different clinics offering abortion services. They staged large-scale anti-abortion protests where they blocked hospitals offering these services to prevent women from obtaining these services. There are numerous anti- abortion demonstrations and the most commonly cited one is the Siege of Atlanta in 1988. During this period, the pro-life protesters engaged in a two day protest where more than 2,500 people were arrested. While these people adopted the use of non-violent means of advocating for an end to abortion, some of these activists started proposing the use of violent methods to ensure that these pro-abortion clinics were shut down (Weitz, 2010). In this case, these groups adopted barbaric methods such as the use of bombs, acid attacks and the burning down of these clinics. These groups also engage in the direct killing of the doctors offering abortion in their clinics. The pro-abortion reacted to the threats and responded to protecting these clinics actively. Fried (2013) indicates that pro- abortion had dedicated themselves in supporting Roe v. Wade. They supported the right to privacy, which was the primary determinant during the court ruling. With the rising tension between the two groups, there was a need to develop the right solution between the two groups. In the development of an amicable solution between the two groups, there was developed of the phrase "Safe, legal, rare." Fried (2013) asserts that the critical anti- abortionist issue is ensuring that the lives of both the woman and the fetus are protected.

After the 1973 decision, the anti-abortionist movement continued to engage in court battles to overturn the decision. Over the years, the anti-abortionist movement through congress has developed different regulations to limit issues related to abortion (Reagan, 2022). Over the years, congress, through the anti-abortion movement, has developed legislation; for example, in 1992, in the case of Planned Parenthood v. Casey, the court had to support the rising number of restrictions. Through the lobby of the anti- abortion movement, the court supported the enactment of several restrictions, such as parental notification and evaluation by the doctor before procuring the abortion. With the persistent anti-abortion movement, one Wednesday 2021, the anti-abortion movement succeeded in banning of abortion among Americans (Reagan, 2022). In this case, even though abortion is still legal in Texas, it is only possible when it happens within the first six weeks. The majority of the regulation related to abortion were made illegal. With the mounting pressure from the anti-abortionist movement, other states adopted the legislation to introduce legislation related to pro-life.

Differences Among Westernized Countries

The debate on abortion and women's reproductive rights has surrounded western countries. In this case, they have developed different laws and regulations regulating issues regarding abortion. Some nations have developed punitive regulations aimed at reducing the number of people acquiring abortions. Some of the nations within Great Britain do not support abortion right among women. Some of these nations include England, Wales and Scotland. Based on their regal framework, they still consider their 1967 Abortion Act. In this case, the Act stipulates that abortion can only be procured when the woman's life is at stake and is defined and signed off by two doctors (Holmes, 2022). In this case, procuring abortion outside the Act might result in imprisonment. The 1967 Act outlined the various issues related to the control of abortion among the people. Some of the conditions related to the Act is that the process must be conducted by a medical practitioner (Journal of Medical Ethics, 2001). The continuation of the pregnancy might potentially cause the loss of the pregnant woman and when the continuation of the pregnancy is associated with greater risk. This is different from the American regulations of abortion, which was perceived as a woman's legal right.

In the UK, one nation that has supported abortion rights is Northern Ireland. The development of abortion rights has faced a series of activism supporting women's rights and ensuring that they decriminalize abortion.

In this case, Northern Ireland has, over time, supported the anti-abortion movement's restrictive regulations (Rough, 2023).

However, over the years, the Northern Ireland Government supported abortion in 2020. In this case, the regulation indicated that one can acquire abortion up to their 12th week gestation period without any form of the condition. When the pregnant woman surpasses the 12th week of their gestation period, it is unlawful to terminate the pregnancy unless under certain conditions, such as fetal abnormalities.

Among the western nations, Canada has adopted a different approach to addressing the issue of abortion among the people. Based on the evaluation, Canada, at the moment, has not enacted any form of regulations related to abortion rights. In 1969, the government supported the procurement of abortion under various conditions. These services were only available in hospitals when a decision by a committee of doctors approved the process, especially in cases where it endangered the woman's life.

Following a series of pro-abortion movements, in 1982, the Canadian government developed the rights and freedoms among the people. In this case, any kind of law found to restrict the freedom of the people was deemed unconstitutional and struck down.

Several years later, in the case of R. v. Morgentaler, in 1988 removed the abortion laws in Canada. It was outlined as unconstitutional in the case since it violated Section seven of the Rights and Freedom charter. One year later, the court also ruled that the father had no legal right to decide on a woman's abortion in 1989 (National Abortion Federation Canada, 2022). Over the years of the introduction of bills and lobbying from the pro-life movement, there is no regulating law related to abortion right in Canada. However, in 2017, there was developed "Safe Access Abortion Services Act" in Ontario. It supports the procurement of abortion at the specified facilities regulated by the providers.

Left and Right Political Viewpoints

American society is polarized between left and right-wing political affiliations. Each of the groups has a different understanding and social beliefs, which play a major role in the development of social politics. They also shape the nation's election since the politicians are elected based on what they believe in. Among the contentious issues that have played out in the USA politics are aborting rights (Kate et al., 2023). The left and right-wing ideologies are based on two key issues; the people's rights and the

government's power. Among the left-wingers, they believe in the liberal understanding. In this case, those in the left-wing indicated that society should be best served with the involvement of the government.

The difference in their approach to these social-political issues differs in every aspect and among them is abortion rights. Based on this understanding, the people in the left support abortion rights. In this case, these people indicated that people should have the liberty to abort when they wish since it is their human right protected under the constitution (Lipka, 2022). Although they support abortion, in some cases, they do not openly express their opinions. Among those in the right wing, they are controlled by their religious beliefs and morality to protect human life. Therefore, these people do not support Roe v. Wade (Kate et al., 2023). They have supported measures to overturn the ruling and ensure that women do not have the free right to engage in abortions when they decide to. In this case, the majority of the right-winged states have developed different regulations to make it hard for women to engage in procuring abortion. In this case, even though abortion is not fully outlawed, they have developed numerous anti-abortion regulations to restrict the procurement of abortion among the people.

The right-wing believes that an unborn child is a living person and that their engagement in abortion violates human life. However, some right-wing people indicated exceptions on issues such as rape cases and incest. On the central, those on the left wing understand that women should have control of their bodies and therefore making abortion illegal violates their rights. They propose that women should enjoy their reproductive rights (Lipka, 2022). The left-wing group also asserts that the infringement of the abortion right would only make women acquire abortion using illegal means when it is not legalized. The failure to legalize abortion is a serious issue that will not reduce the number of people procuring abortions. It only makes the women acquire these services from unqualified underground people, which is a serious health issue (Kate et al., 2023). The failure to have trained professionals offering these services might result in cases of botched abortion cases that might affect the health of the women and also result in the loss of lives among the people.

Lipka (2022) also asserts that people who are opposed to abortion are those in the religious setting. Based on the evaluation, most people are Christians; about 57% are Protestants, 23% are Catholics and about 3% are from the Church of Jesus Christ. Based on the evaluation, religious commitment among the people has played a major role in making people commit their effort not supporting abortion (Lipka, 2022). They indicate that abortion should be illegal and immorally taking an individual's life. The higher religious commitment has played a major in their beliefs concerning abortion.

CONCLUSION

In conclusion, abortion is a serious issue that has affected society differently. Different groups in the debate offer differing information concerning either the objection or the support of abortion. Within the American context, there are numerous legal battles that people have engaged to ensure that their opinions are legalized. Some of the critical issues include the moral status and the legal right of women in making decisions related to abortion. Based on the historical account, the case of abortion within the American context started in the 1800s when the American indigenous people adopted a different measure to produce abortion (Acevedo, 1979). Some of the issues they used included the use of herbal medicine and crude ways of acquiring an abortion. During the colonial period, people were regulated by the rule of the colonials, where the British people used their laws and it was illegal to engage in abortion.

One of the grand rulings that shaped the discourse of abortion is the issue of Roe v. Wade. In the grand ruling, they relied on the right to privacy as the primary reason for accepting abortion rights. In this case, it allowed the women to terminate their pregnancies (Linton, 1989). Although there was the adoption of the legislation, numerous people objected to the idea. In this case, numerous people joined hands to form the anti- abortion movement (Weitz, 2010). Further, the issue of abortion led to the development of both right and left-wing groups in the American context. The left-wing support abortion and the right-wing object to the ideology of abortion unless under certain specification. They believe that the fetus is a living human and that life should be protected.

ABOUT THE AUTHOR

Dorris Woods is a native of Mississippi. After graduating at the top of her high school class, she left to go to work in Des Moines, Iowa. Her family did not have money for college.

After working for about a year, her break came when cousin Carrie told her about a nursing school in Atlanta, Georgia. She applied and was accepted to the Grady Memorial Hospital School of Nursing. She likes the quote: "Atlanta Can't Live Without Grady".

Dr. Woods began her career as a pediatric charge nurse at Grady. After completing state board exams, she went to work at Children's Hospital in Chicago in Nursing Administration. She left after two years to attend Indiana University in Bloomington, another recommendation by Cousin Carrie. She married her husband, Burton, upon graduation; they moved to California.

Since that time, she has earned a second Bachelor of Science degree in psychology from NYU, a Master's degree in Counseling at Cal State University, a double Master's degree at UCLA, one in pediatrics/administration, the other in mental health. She later earned a doctorate from Claremont Graduate University. Post-doctoral work was completed at UCLA. She "loves the classroom". She ranks at the eight-eight percentile of people educated in America.

Dr. Woods began her writing with the book, *Breaking Point: Fighting to End American's Teenage Suicide Epidemic!* which was based on her doctoral dissertation research. She has written many articles on the topic and conducted workshops. Her second book, *How to Prevent Diabetes–I Beat it and You Can, Too*! was written to inform a large public unsuspecting of the problems and a solution. Her third book, *Abortion and The Senseless Assault on Reproductive Rights!* also written in the public interest was motivated by the egregious act of overturning Roe v. Wade which has caused undue trauma to women and taken medical decision out of the hands of physicians.

Dr. Woods is a widow. She is the mother of three children and lives in Culver City, California.

REFERENCES

Ahmed, T., North Dakota governor signs law banning abortion at 6 weeks. April 24, 2023.

American Civil Liberties Union, "Know your rights: Abortion access in California: ACLU of Northern CA. ACLU of Northern California, 2023.

Associated Press, "Women sue Texas, saying abortion ban put their lives at risk," *Los Angeles Times,* March 8, 2023, p. 16.

Bansode, O.M.,Sarao, M.S.,& Cooper, D.B. Contraception, 2022.

Barnes, Robert and Lumpkin, Lauren, "Alito reluctant to discuss state of Supreme Court after Roe leak," *Washington Post,* May 12, 2022.

Brindis, C.D., Decker, M.J., Guttmann-Gonzalez, A., & Berglas, N.F. "Perspectives on adolescent pregnancy prevention strategies in the United States: looking back, looking forward." *Adolescent health, medicine and therapeutics,* 135-145, 2020.

Britton, L.E., Alspaugh, A., Greene, M.Z., & McLemore, M.R., "An Evidence-Based Update on Contraception: A detailed review of Hormonal and non-hormonal methods." *The American Journal of Nursing*, 120(2), 2020.

Calimag, M. M.P., Gamilla, M.C.Z., & Aubrey, E., Natural Family Planning Methods: A Scoping Review, *Journal of Social Health*, 3(1), 2020.

Calmes, Jackie, "Here's action to take on Clarence Thomas' ever-expanding ethics scandal," *Los Angeles Times,* p. A11, May 6, 2023.

Clarity Cares, 10 tips to handle temptation. https://claritycares.org/10-tips-handle- temptation/, 2016.

Cleveland Clinic, Pull-out method (withdrawal): Effectiveness & Risks, 2023a.

Craven, Jessica, "Chief Justice Roberts, stop the rot," Letters to the Editor, *Los Angeles Times,* April 18, 2023.

D'Innocenzio, Anne and Alexandra Olson, "Abortion bans put low-wage workers in financial bind," *Associated Press/Los Angeles Times,* Saturday, November 5, 2022, p. A12.

Donegan, M., The anti-abortion movement just had a mask-off moment in Alabama; Moira Donegan, *The Guardian,* January 13, 2023.

Easters, M. "Georgia has long history for progressive abortion policies", *Georgia WIN List,* May 4, 2022.

Findlaw, "Alabama abortion laws - findlaw, *FindLaw,* 2022. Findlaw, "New Jersey Abortion Laws - Findlaw", *Findlaw,* 2022.

Flaws, S.I. "New name, same harm: Rebranding of federal abstinence-only programs, *Guttmacher Policy Review, 21,* 2018.

Goldberg, Nicholas, "After 50 years, abortion rights are set back to zero," *Los Angeles Times,* Thursday, January 19, 2023, p. A11.

Guttmacher Institute, "Interactive map: U.S. abortion policies and access after Roe", *Guttmacher Institute,* 2022.

Henneberg, Christine, "The over-the-counter birth control pill is a hollow victory," *Los Angeles Times,* OP-ED, July 19, 2023, p. A13.

Holom-Trundy, B., "What the Dobbs Decision Means for abortion rights in New Jersey and beyond - new jersey policy perspective, *New Jersey Policy Perspective,* December 19, 2022.

Hurt, E. "How Georgia's anti-abortion law has affected the abortion rate", 2023.

Hwang, K. "How California created the nation's easiest abortion access - and why it's going further", *CalMatters,* April 21, 2022.

Jalonick, Mary Clare and Sherman, Mark and Freking, Kevin, "Roberts won't testify on Supreme Court's ethics for Senate panel, *Associated Press/Los Angeles Times,* April 26, 2023, p. A9.

Kaiser Family Foundation, "Natural family planning as a means of preventing pregnancy", August 15, 2018.

Kaneshiro, B., & Aeby, T., "Long-term safety, efficacy, and patient acceptability of the intrauterine Copper T-380A contraceptive device", *International Journal of Women's Health,* 211-220, 2010.

Kekatos, M., "North Dakota Supreme Court says state abortion ban is 'unconstitutional', *ABC News,* 2023.

Lipttak, Adam, "The Supreme Court Public Opinion and the Fate of Roe," *The New York Times National,* Tuesday, June 21, 2022, p. 18.

Lyman, B., & Mealins, E., "A history of abortion law and abortion access in Alabama", *Montgomery Adviser,* June 24, 2022.

Malady, H., Shaeffer, A.D., & McNabb, D.M. "Condoms", 2023 Marino, S., Canela, D.C., & Nama, N., "Tubal Sterilization", 2022.

Mayo Clinic, Depo-Provera, (contraceptive injection), February 22, 2022a.

Mejia, Brittny, "Abortion Pill may be revealing," *Los Angeles Times* Headlines, April 18, 2023.

Mejia, Brittny, "How the LAPD abortion squad went after women and doctors in the pre-Roe era," *Los Angeles Times,* pp1, 10-11, Sunday, April 2, 2023.

Mome, R.K., Wiyeh, A.B., Kongnyuy, U.J., & Wiysonge, C.S., "Effectiveness of female condom in preventing HIV and sexually transmitted infections: a systematic review protocol", *BMJ open,* 8(8), e023055, 2018.

New Jersey Office of the Attorney General, "New Jersey Office of the attorney general know your rights abortion...New Jersey Office of the Attorney General", https://www.nj.gov/oag/library/2022/Know-Your-Rights-Abortion-Rights-06-30-22, pdf., 2022.

NPR, "Georgia's highest Court reinstates ban on abortion after 6 weeks", NPR, https://www.npr.org/2022/11/23/1139039767/georgia-supreme-court-reinstates- abortion-ban, November 23, 2022.

Nguyen, N., Nguyen, L., Nguyen, H., & Gallo, M.F., "Correlates of use of withdrawal for contraception among women in Vietnam", *BMC Women's Health,* 20, 1-7, 2020.

OHCHR, "United States: Abortion bans put millions of women and girls at risk, U.N. experts say", OHCHR, https://www.ohchr.org/en/press-releases/2023/06/united-   states-abortion-bans-put-millions-women-and-girls-risk-un-experts-say, June 2, 2023.

Pendleton, B. "The California Therapeutic Abortion Act: An Analysis", *Hastings LJ, 19, 242,* 1967.

Perrone, Matthew, "Landmark birth control pill Oked," *Los Angeles Times,* p. A1, July 14, 2023.

Planned Parenthood, "What is the effectiveness of spermicide?" 2023c.

Procaccini, Francesca and Guggenberger, Nikolas, "Angry about the Supreme Court? Blame Congress, *Los Angeles Times,* OP-ED, p. A21, July 6, 2023.

Ridgeway, K., Montgomery, E.T., Smith, K., Torjesen, K., van der Straten, A., Achilles, S.L., & Griffin, J.B., "Vaginal ring acceptability:

A systematic review and meta- analysis of vaginal ring experiences from around the world, *Contraception, 106,* 16-33, 2022.

Rogin, A., & Young, K., "The state of abortion access in America a year after Roe's reversal", *PBS,* June 24, 2 023.

SHOUSE LAW GROUP, "California abortion laws - what you need to know post-roe", Shouse Law Group, https://www/shouselaw. com/ca/defense/laws/abortion-laws/, December 30, 2022.

Smith, M.H., Muzyezka, Z., Chakraborty, P., Johns-Wolfe, E., Higgins, J., Bessett, D., & Norris, A.H., "Abortion travel within the United States: an observational study of cross-state movement to obtain abortion care in 2017", *The Lancet Regional Health- Americas, 10,* 2022.

Smith, T.E., Panisch, L.S., Malespin, T., & Pereira, M.G., "Evaluating effectiveness of abstinence education", *Journal of Evidence-Informed Social Work, 14*(5), 360-367.

State of California, "In response to Supreme Court decision Governor Newsom signs legislation to protect women and providers in California from abortion bans by other states", June 25, 2022.

Stormont, G., & Deibert, C.M., "Vasectomy", 2023.

Sung, S., & Abramovitz, A., "Natural family planning", 2019.

Taranto, James and Rirkin, David Jr., Justice "Samuel Alito: This Made Us Targets of Assassination," *Opinion, The Weekend Interview,* April 29, 2023.

The New York Times, "Tracking the states where abortion is banned", *The New York Times,* May 24, 2022.

Treisman, R., "States with the toughest abortion laws have the weakest maternal supports", *Data Shows, NPR,* August 18, 2022.

Van Sickle, Abbie, Prominent Retired Judge Calls for Ethics Rules for Supreme Court Justices, *New York Times,* May 2, 2023.

Wagner, John, "Senator Durbin invites Roberts to testify on Supreme Court ethics amid Thomas Revelations," *Washington Post,* April 20, 2023.

White, A.L., Davis, R.E., Billings, D.L., & Mann, E.S., "Men's vasectomy knowledge, attitudes, and information-seeking behaviors in the Southern United States: results from an exploratory survey", *American Journal of Men's Health, 14*(4), 2020.

Zuniga, C., Blanchard, K., Harper, C.C., Wollum, A., Key, K., & Henderson, J.T., "Effectiveness and efficacy rates of progestin-only pills: A comprehensive literature review", 2022.

REFERENCES

(BACK STORY ON ABORTION)

Acevedo, Z. (1979). Abortion in early America. *Women & Health,* 4(2), 159-167. Doi:10.1300/J013v04n04_05.

Beckman, L. J. (2017). Abortion in the United States: The continuing controversy.

Feminism & Psychology, 27(1), 101-113. https://doi. org/10.1177/0959353516685345

Fried, M. G. (2013). Reproductive rights activism in the post-Roe era. *American Journal of Public Health,* 103(1), 10-14.

Holmes, N. (2022). Evidence-based abortion care: how Roe v Wade highlights the need for quality research in the UK and beyond. *Midirs midwifery digest,* 32(4), 406-408. https://researchonline. lshtm.ac.uk/id/eprint/4668294/1/Salaria_2022_Evidence-based-abortion-care.pdf

Journal of Medical Ethics, (2001). About abortion in Britain. http://dx/ doi.org/10.1136/jme.27.suppl_2.ii33

Kate T., Gauri S., Nathan J. Brauer, Nikhilesh Jasuja, Saris, William Olive, Tom Rosta, Casey Lee, Teresa Mayer, B, Ian Baker (2023. "Left Wing vs Right Wing." *Diffen.com*. Diffen LLC, n.d. Web. 27 Feb 2023. <https://www.diffen.com/difference/Left_Wing_vs_Right_Wing>

Lipka, M. (2022, June 17). *A closer look at Republicans who favor legal abortion and Democrats who oppose it*. Pew Research Center. Retrieved March 8, 2023, from https://www.pewresearch. org/fact-tank/2022/06/17/a-closer-look-at-republicans-who- favor-legal-abortion-and-democrats-who-oppose-it/

Linton, P. B. (1989). Roe v. Wade and the history of abortion regulation. *American Journal of Law & Medicine, 15*(2-3), 227-233.

National Abortion Federation Canada. (2022). *History of abortion in Canada*. National Abortion Federation Canada. Retrieved March 8, 2023, from https://nafcanada.org/history-abortion-canada/

Rough, (2023) Abortion in Northern Ireland: recent changes to the legal framework https://researchbriefings.files.parliament.uk/documents/CBP-8909/CBP-8909.pdf

Reagan, L. J. (2022). *When Abortion Was a Crime: Women, Medicine, and Law in the United States. 1867-1973, with a New Preface*. Univ of California Press.

Sauer, R. (1974). Attitudes to abortion in America, 1800-1973. *Population Studies, 28*(1), 53-67. https://doi. org/10.1080/003247 28.1974.10404578

Warren, M. A. (2017). On the moral and legal status of abortion. In *Applied Ethics* (pp. 360-367). Routledge. https://amberhinds.com/2p-content/uploads/2012/01/warren-   moralandlegalstatusofabortion. pdf

Weitz, T. A. (2016). Rethinking the mantra that abortion should be "safe, legal and rare". *Journal of women's history*, 22(3), 161-172.

www.ingramcontent.com/pod-product-compliance
Lightning Source LLC
Chambersburg PA
CBHW031902200326
41597CB00012B/517